ANGEL™

Surrogates

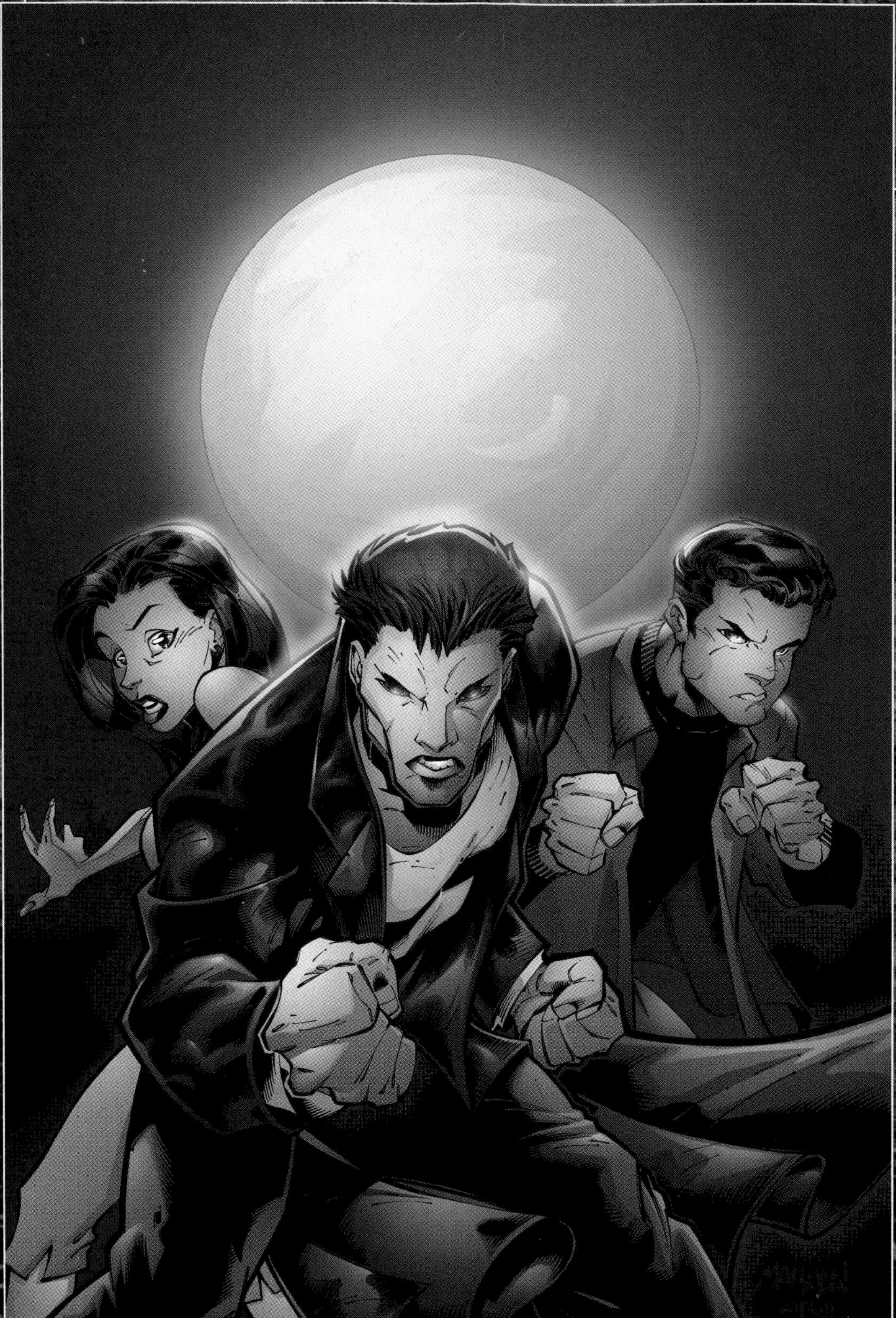

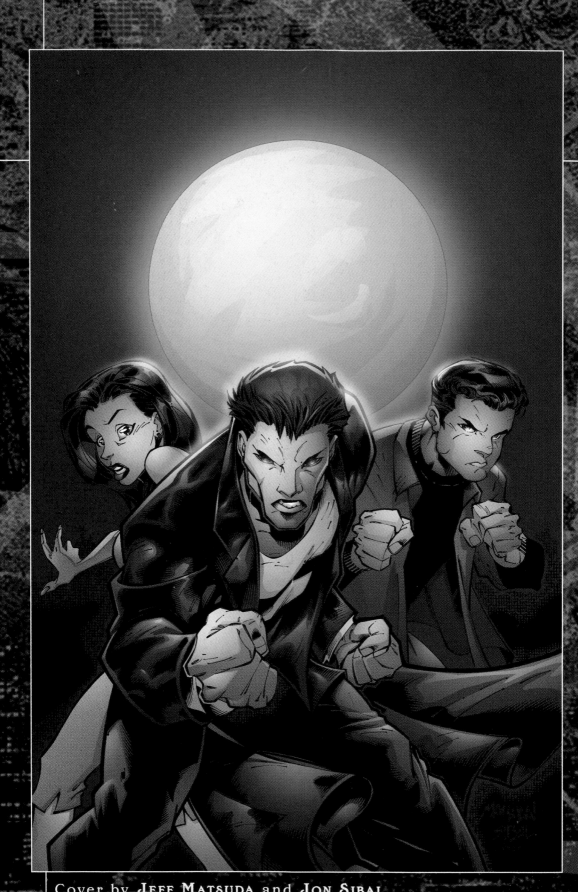

Cover by Jeff Matsuda and Jon Sibal
Colors by Guy Major

ANGEL ™

Surrogates

based on the television series
created by
JOSS WHEDON and DAVID GREENWALT

writer
CHRISTOPHER GOLDEN

penciller
CHRISTIAN ZANIER

pencil assists
MARVIN MARIANO

inker
ANDY OWENS
with JASON MINOR and CURTIS P. ARNOLD

colorist
GUY MAJOR

letterers
CLEM ROBINS and AMADOR CISNEROS

Titan Books

publisher
MIKE RICHARDSON

editor
SCOTT ALLIE
with ADAM GALLARDO

collection designer
KEITH WOOD

art director
MARK COX

Special thanks to
DEBBIE OLSHAN at Fox Licensing,
CAROLINE KALLAS and GEORGE SNYDER at
Buffy the Vampire Slayer.

Published by
Titan Books
144 Southwark Street
London SE1 OUP

First edition: February 2001
ISBN: 1-84023-234-X

1 3 5 7 9 10 8 6 4 2

Printed in Canada.
This story takes place during *Angel's* first season.

What did you think of this book? We love to hear from our readers. Please e-mail us at
readerfeedback@titanemail.com or write to Reader Feedback at the address above.

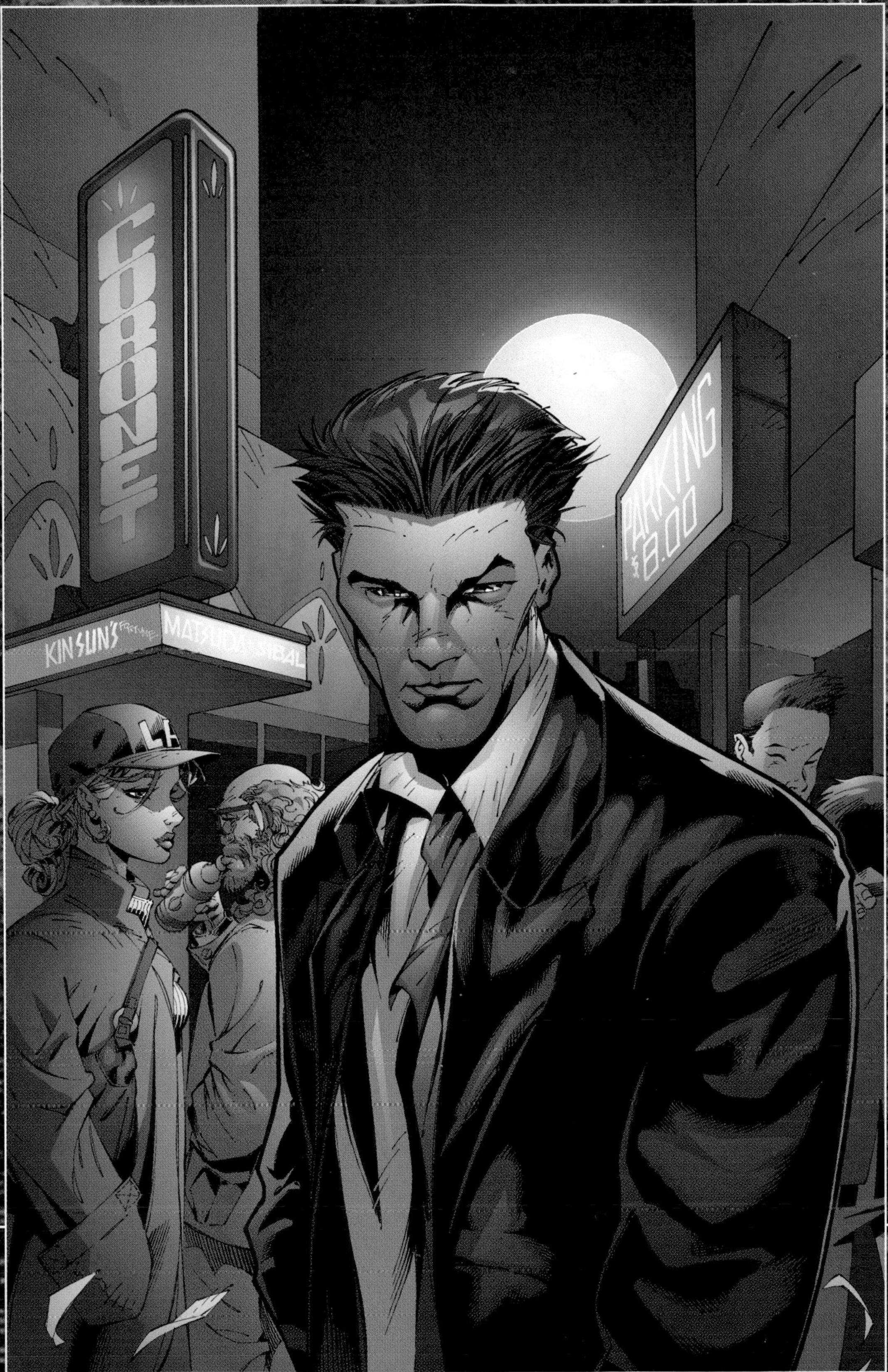
CORONET
KIN SUN'S
MATSUDA & SIBAL
PARKING
$8.00
LA

Cover by **JEFF MATSUDA** and **JON SIBAL**
Colors by **GUY MAJOR**

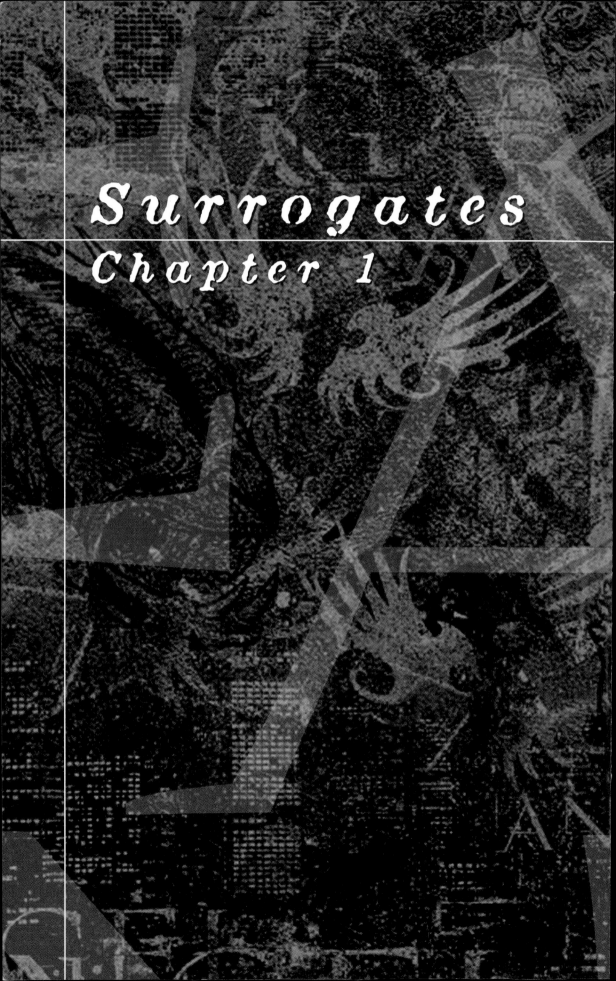

Surrogates
Chapter 1

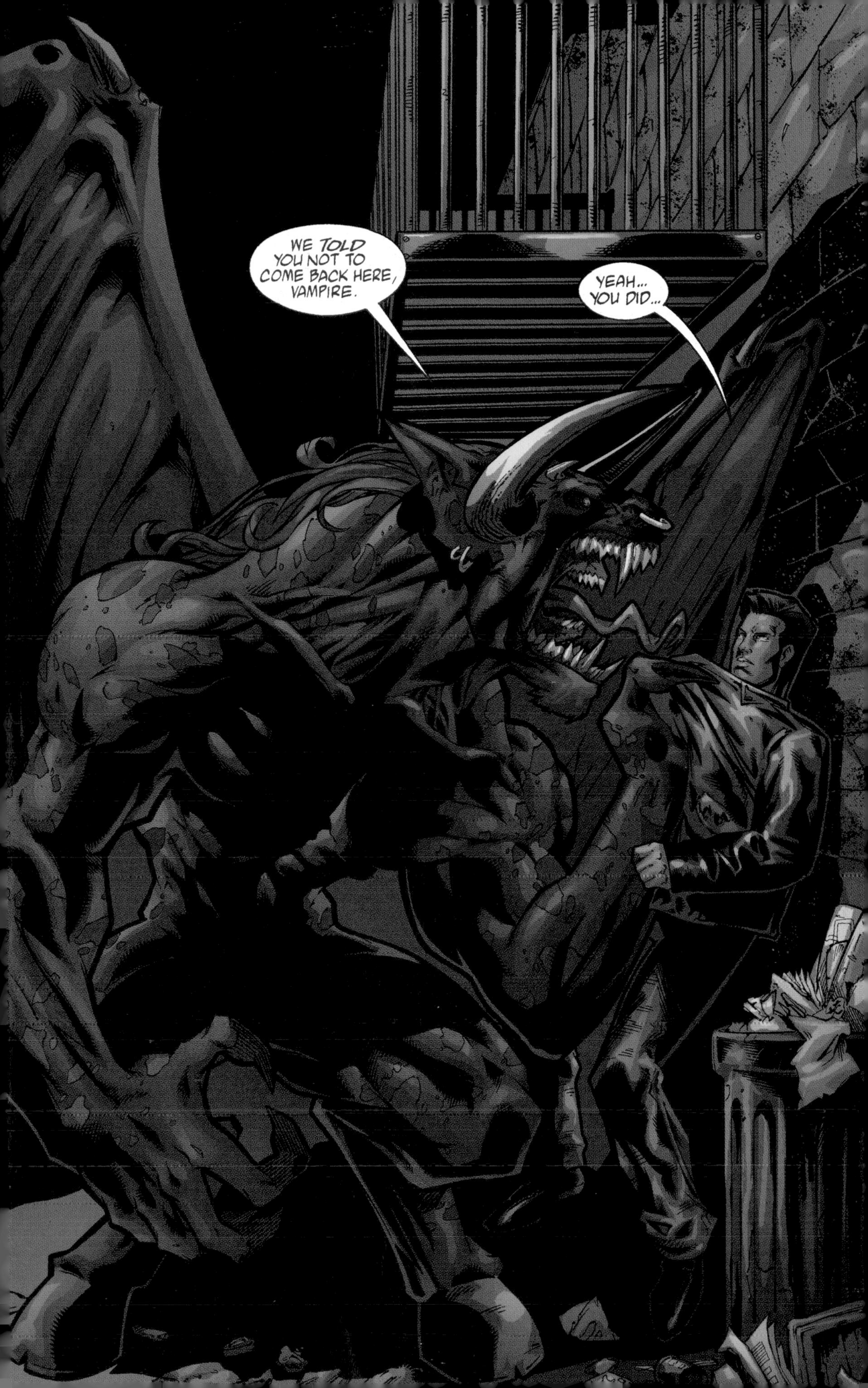
WE TOLD YOU NOT TO COME BACK HERE, VAMPIRE.
YEAH... YOU DID...

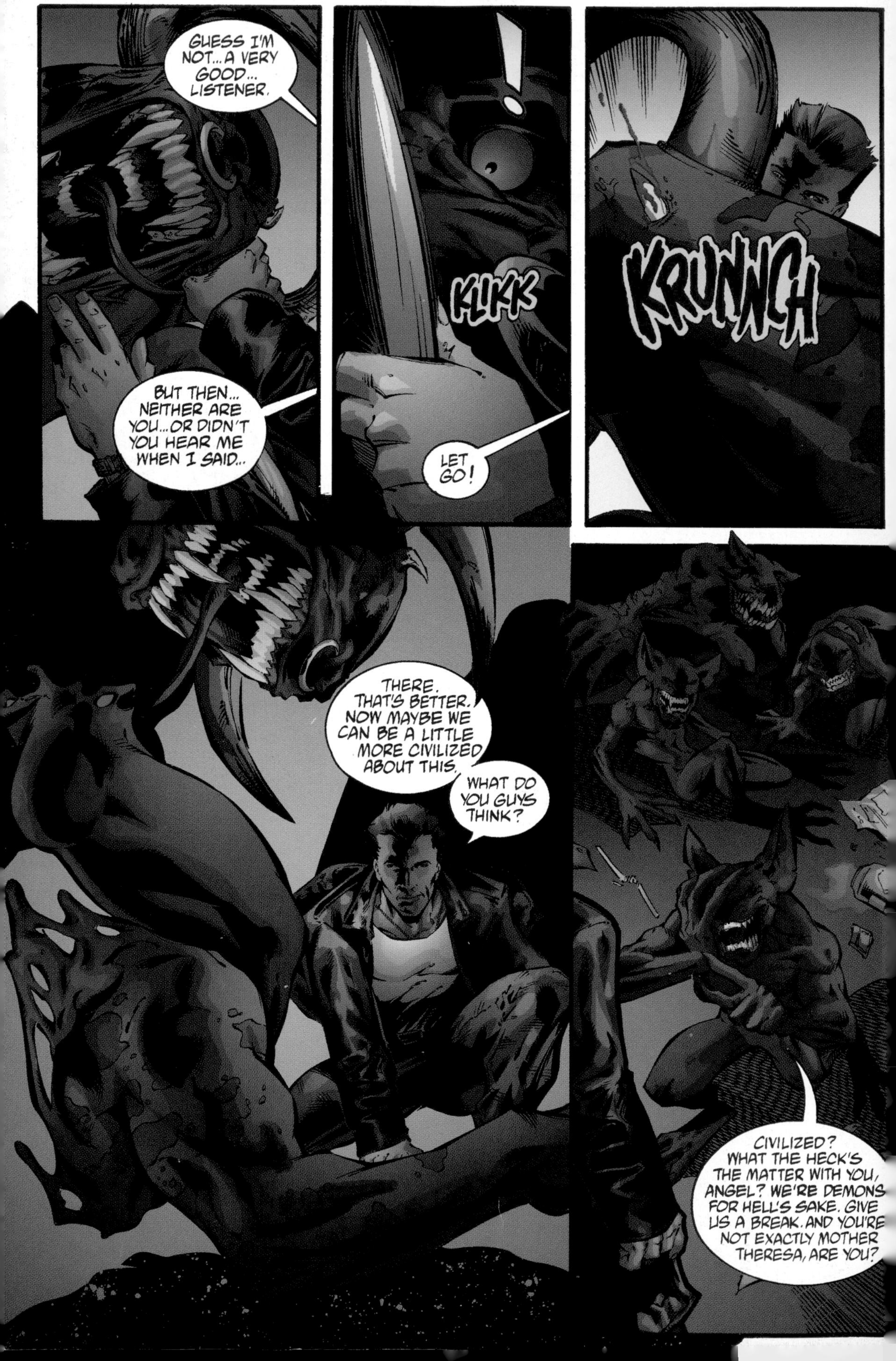
GUESS I'M NOT...A VERY GOOD... LISTENER.
BUT THEN... NEITHER ARE YOU...OR DIDN'T YOU HEAR ME WHEN I SAID...
!
KLIKK
LET GO!
KRUNNCH
THERE. THAT'S BETTER. NOW MAYBE WE CAN BE A LITTLE MORE CIVILIZED ABOUT THIS.
WHAT DO YOU GUYS THINK?
CIVILIZED? WHAT THE HECK'S THE MATTER WITH YOU, ANGEL? WE'RE DEMONS FOR HELL'S SAKE. GIVE US A BREAK. AND YOU'RE NOT EXACTLY MOTHER THERESA, ARE YOU?

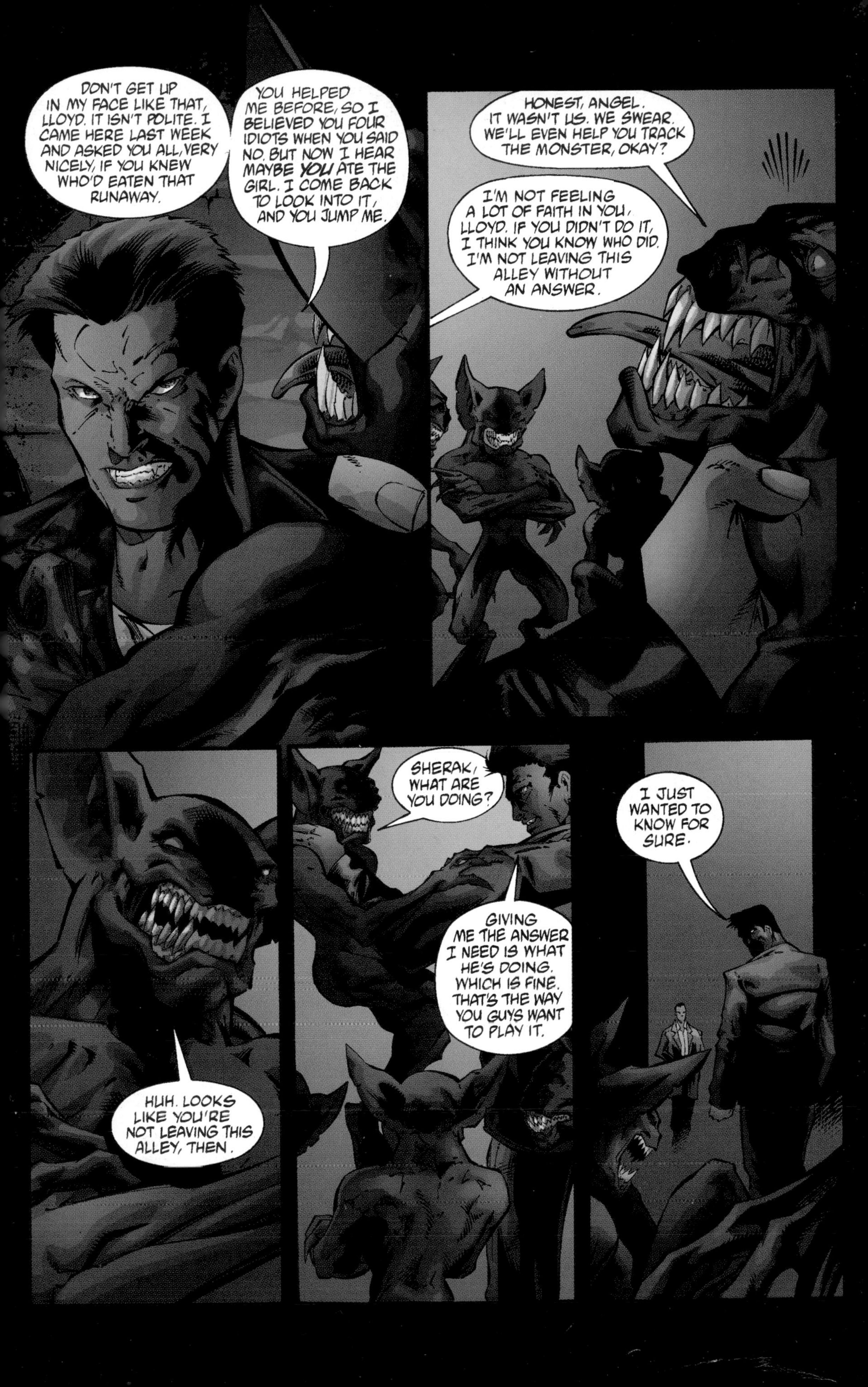
DON'T GET UP IN MY FACE LIKE THAT, LLOYD. IT ISN'T POLITE. I CAME HERE LAST WEEK AND ASKED YOU ALL, VERY NICELY, IF YOU KNEW WHO'D EATEN THAT RUNAWAY.
YOU HELPED ME BEFORE, SO I BELIEVED YOU FOUR IDIOTS WHEN YOU SAID NO. BUT NOW I HEAR MAYBE *YOU* ATE THE GIRL. I COME BACK TO LOOK INTO IT, AND YOU JUMP ME.
HONEST, ANGEL. IT WASN'T US. WE SWEAR. WE'LL EVEN HELP YOU TRACK THE MONSTER, OKAY?
I'M NOT FEELING A LOT OF FAITH IN YOU, LLOYD. IF YOU DIDN'T DO IT, I THINK YOU KNOW WHO DID. I'M NOT LEAVING THIS ALLEY WITHOUT AN ANSWER.
HUH. LOOKS LIKE YOU'RE NOT LEAVING THIS ALLEY, THEN.
SHERAK, WHAT ARE YOU DOING?
GIVING ME THE ANSWER I NEED IS WHAT HE'S DOING. WHICH IS FINE. THAT'S THE WAY YOU GUYS WANT TO PLAY IT.
I JUST WANTED TO KNOW FOR SURE.

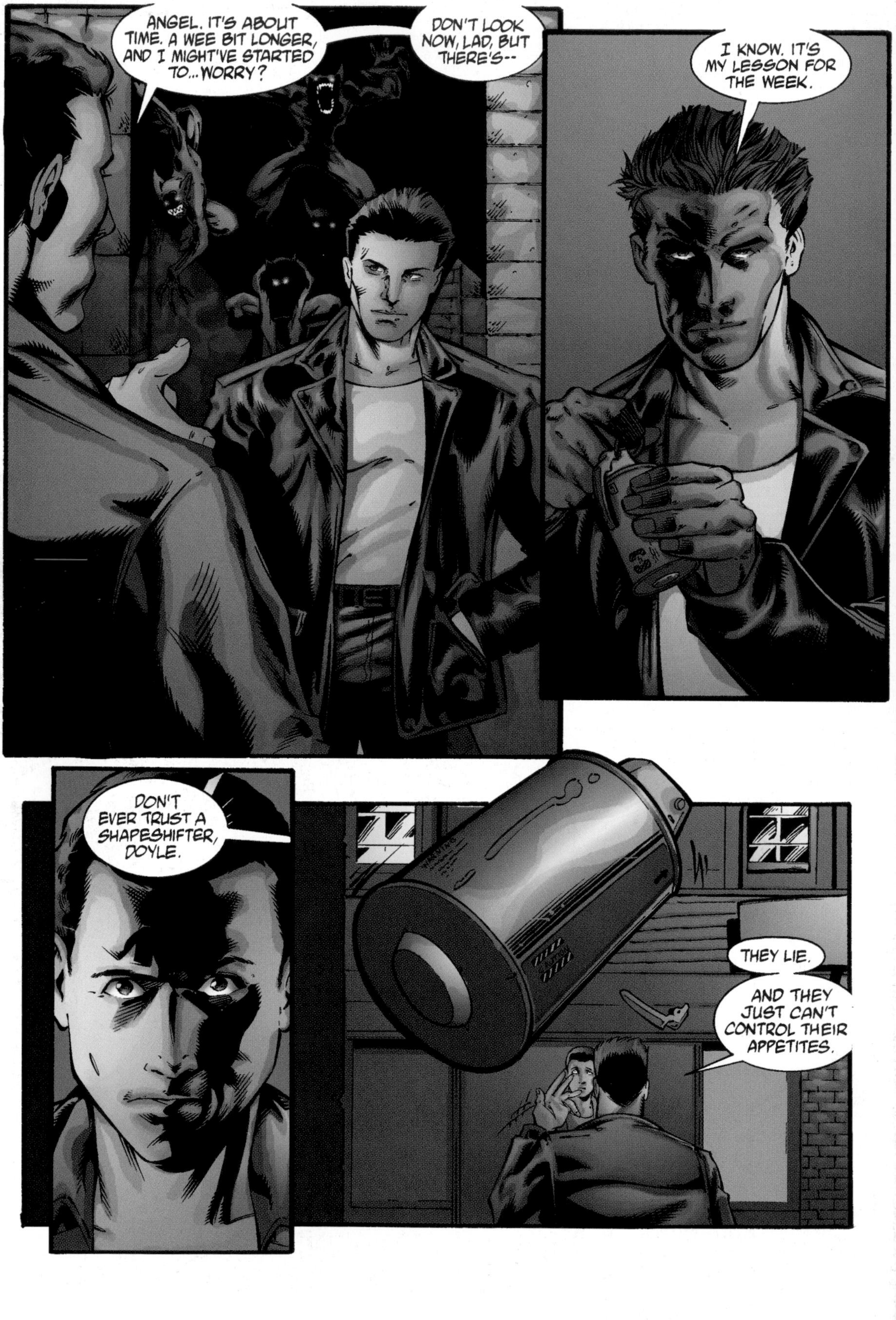
ANGEL. IT'S ABOUT TIME. A WEE BIT LONGER, AND I MIGHT'VE STARTED TO... WORRY?
DON'T LOOK NOW, LAD, BUT THERE'S--
I KNOW. IT'S MY LESSON FOR THE WEEK.
DON'T EVER TRUST A SHAPESHIFTER, DOYLE.
THEY LIE.
AND THEY JUST CAN'T CONTROL THEIR APPETITES.

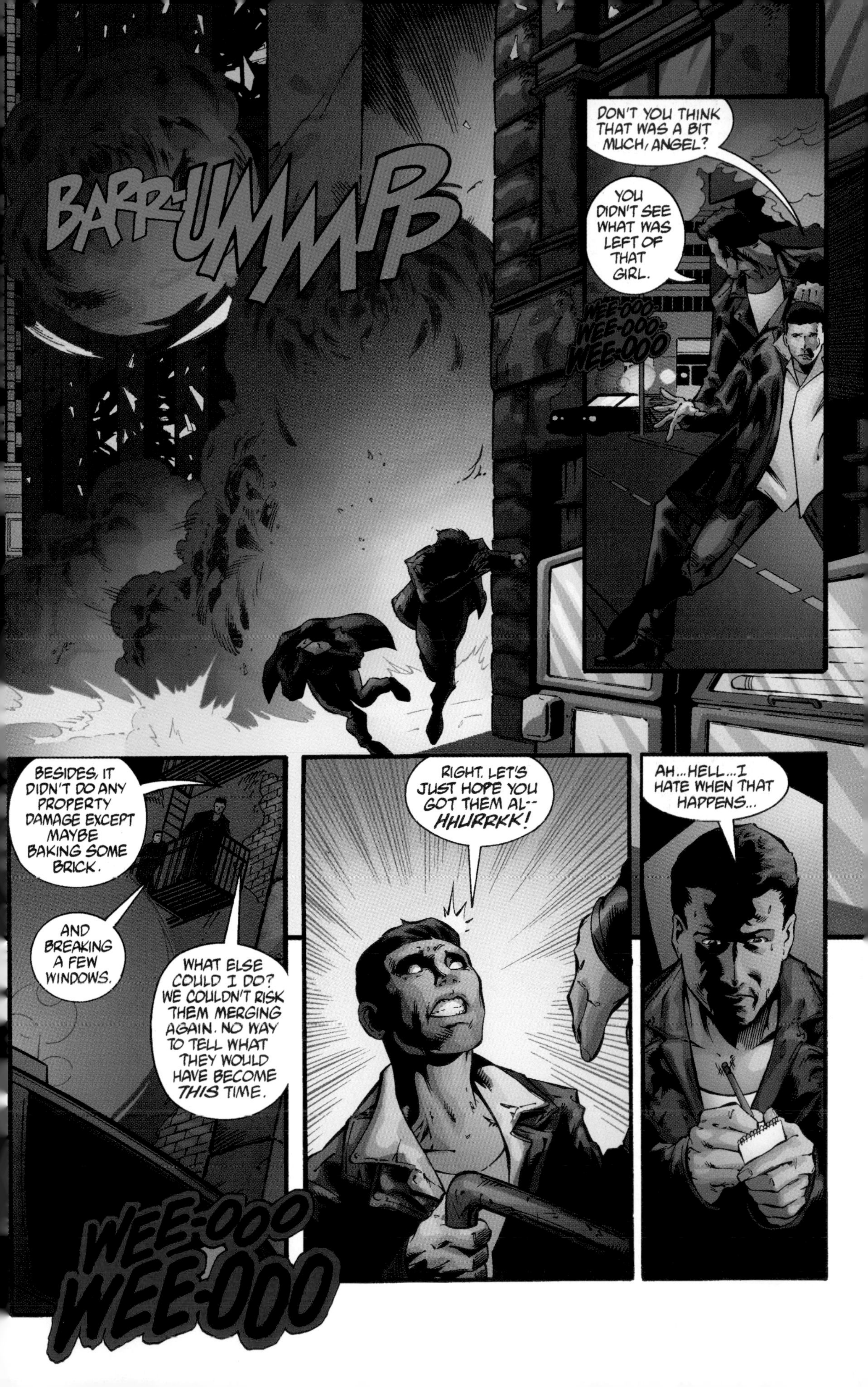
BARR-UMMMB
DON'T YOU THINK THAT WAS A BIT MUCH, ANGEL?
YOU DIDN'T SEE WHAT WAS LEFT OF THAT GIRL.
WEE-OOO-WEE-OOO-WEE-OOO
BESIDES, IT DIDN'T DO ANY PROPERTY DAMAGE EXCEPT MAYBE BAKING SOME BRICK.
AND BREAKING A FEW WINDOWS.
WHAT ELSE COULD I DO? WE COULDN'T RISK THEM MERGING AGAIN. NO WAY TO TELL WHAT THEY WOULD HAVE BECOME THIS TIME.
RIGHT. LET'S JUST HOPE YOU GOT THEM AL--HHURRKK!
AH...HELL...I HATE WHEN THAT HAPPENS...
WEE-OOO WEE-OOO

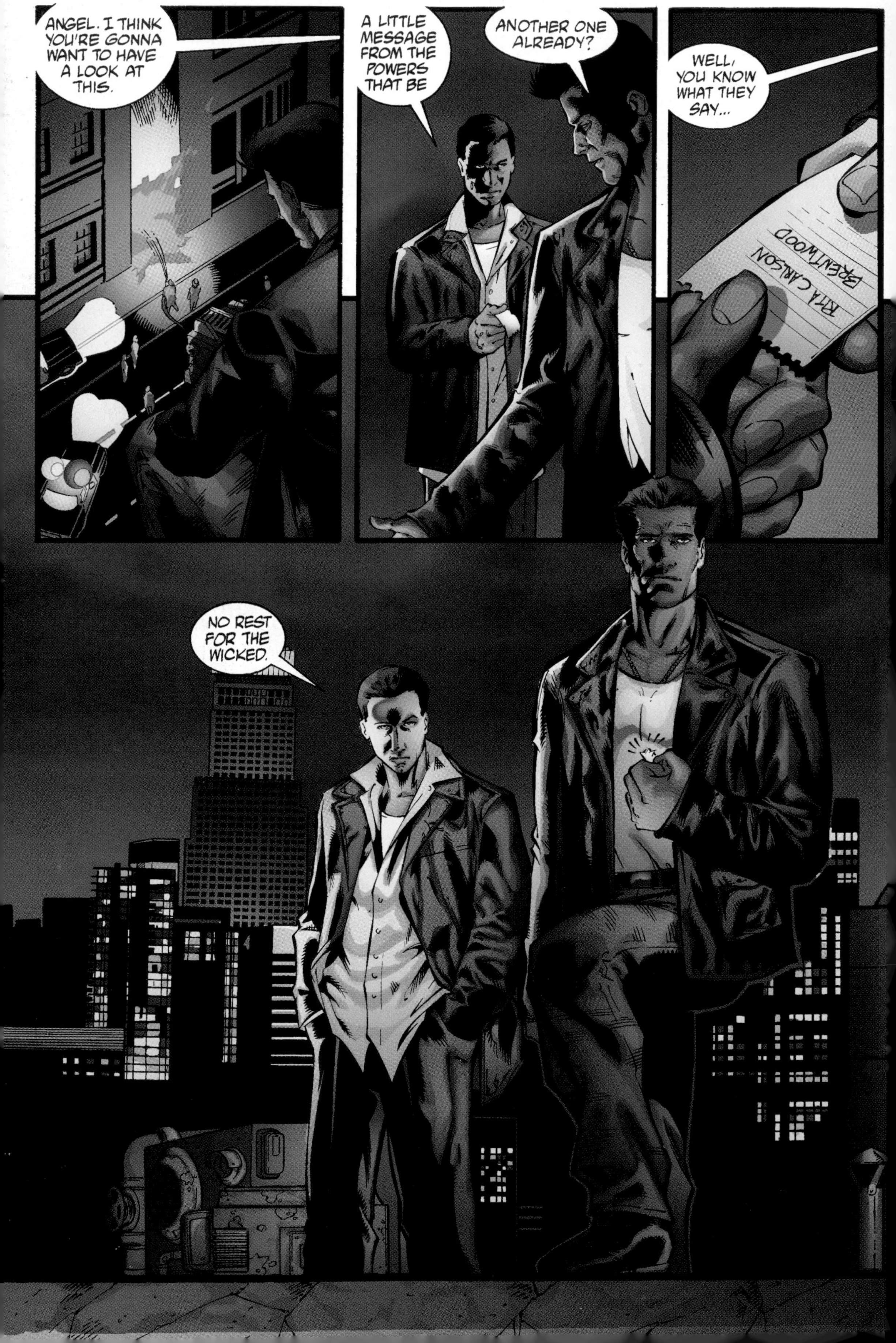
ANGEL. I THINK YOU'RE GONNA WANT TO HAVE A LOOK AT THIS.
A LITTLE MESSAGE FROM THE POWERS THAT BE
ANOTHER ONE ALREADY?
WELL, YOU KNOW WHAT THEY SAY...
RITA CARLSON
BRENTWOOD
NO REST FOR THE WICKED.

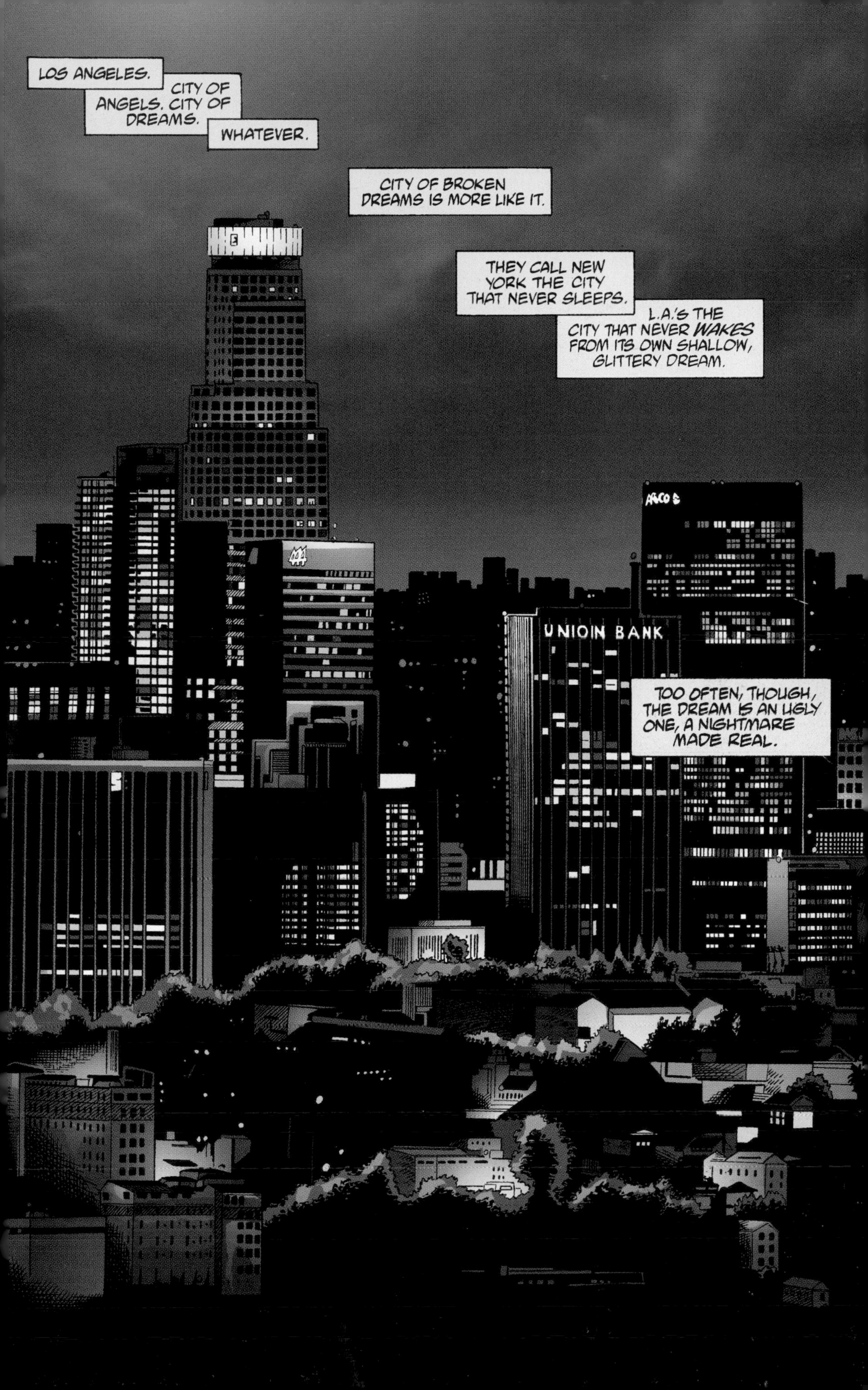
LOS ANGELES.
CITY OF ANGELS. CITY OF DREAMS.
WHATEVER.
CITY OF BROKEN DREAMS IS MORE LIKE IT.
THEY CALL NEW YORK THE CITY THAT NEVER SLEEPS.
L.A.'S THE CITY THAT NEVER WAKES FROM ITS OWN SHALLOW, GLITTERY DREAM.
UNION BANK
TOO OFTEN, THOUGH, THE DREAM IS AN UGLY ONE, A NIGHTMARE MADE REAL.

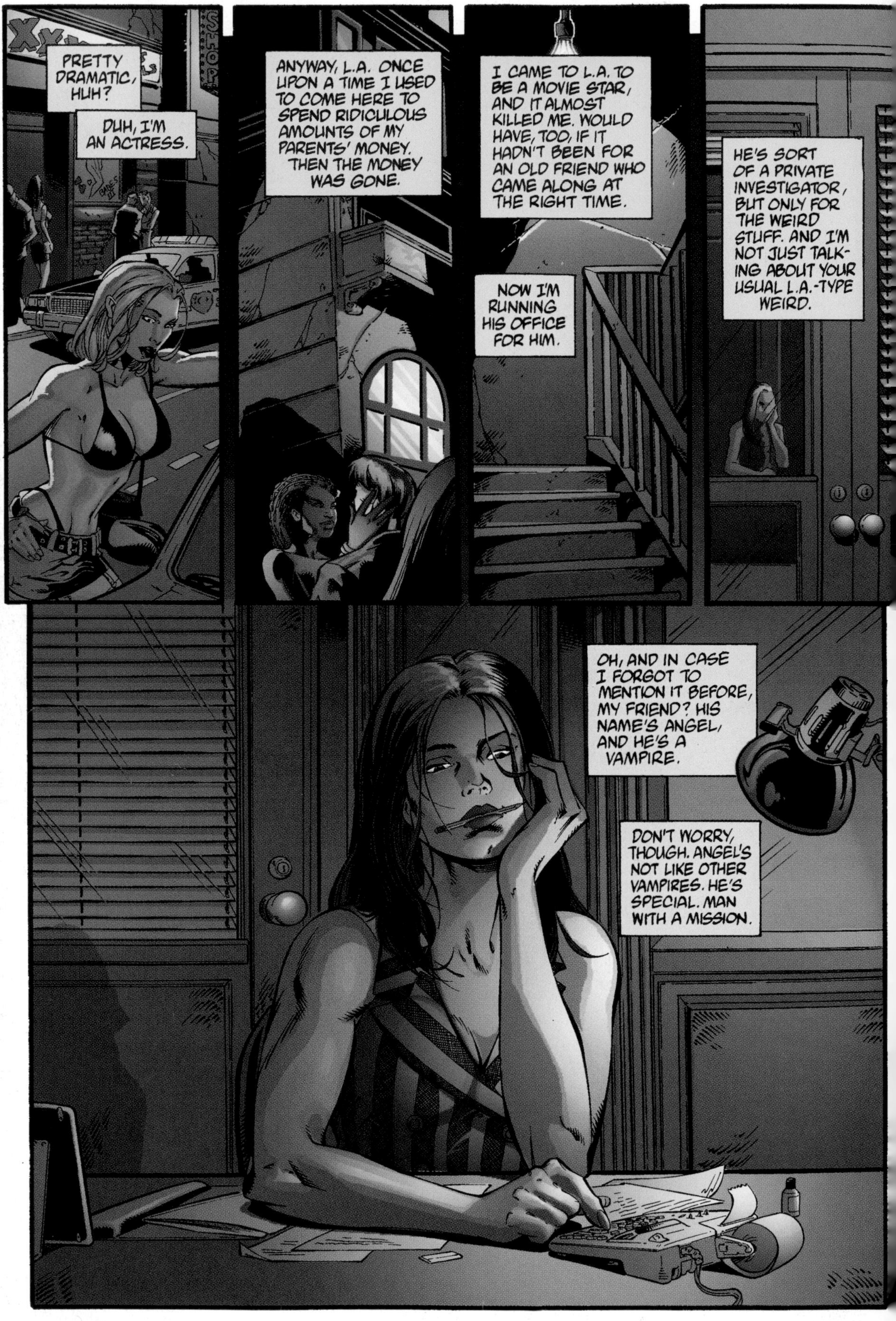
PRETTY DRAMATIC, HUH?
DUH, I'M AN ACTRESS.
ANYWAY, L.A. ONCE UPON A TIME I USED TO COME HERE TO SPEND RIDICULOUS AMOUNTS OF MY PARENTS' MONEY. THEN THE MONEY WAS GONE.
I CAME TO L.A. TO BE A MOVIE STAR, AND IT ALMOST KILLED ME. WOULD HAVE, TOO, IF IT HADN'T BEEN FOR AN OLD FRIEND WHO CAME ALONG AT THE RIGHT TIME.
NOW I'M RUNNING HIS OFFICE FOR HIM.
HE'S SORT OF A PRIVATE INVESTIGATOR, BUT ONLY FOR THE WEIRD STUFF. AND I'M NOT JUST TALKING ABOUT YOUR USUAL L.A.-TYPE WEIRD.
OH, AND IN CASE I FORGOT TO MENTION IT BEFORE, MY FRIEND? HIS NAME'S ANGEL, AND HE'S A VAMPIRE.
DON'T WORRY, THOUGH. ANGEL'S NOT LIKE OTHER VAMPIRES. HE'S SPECIAL. MAN WITH A MISSION.

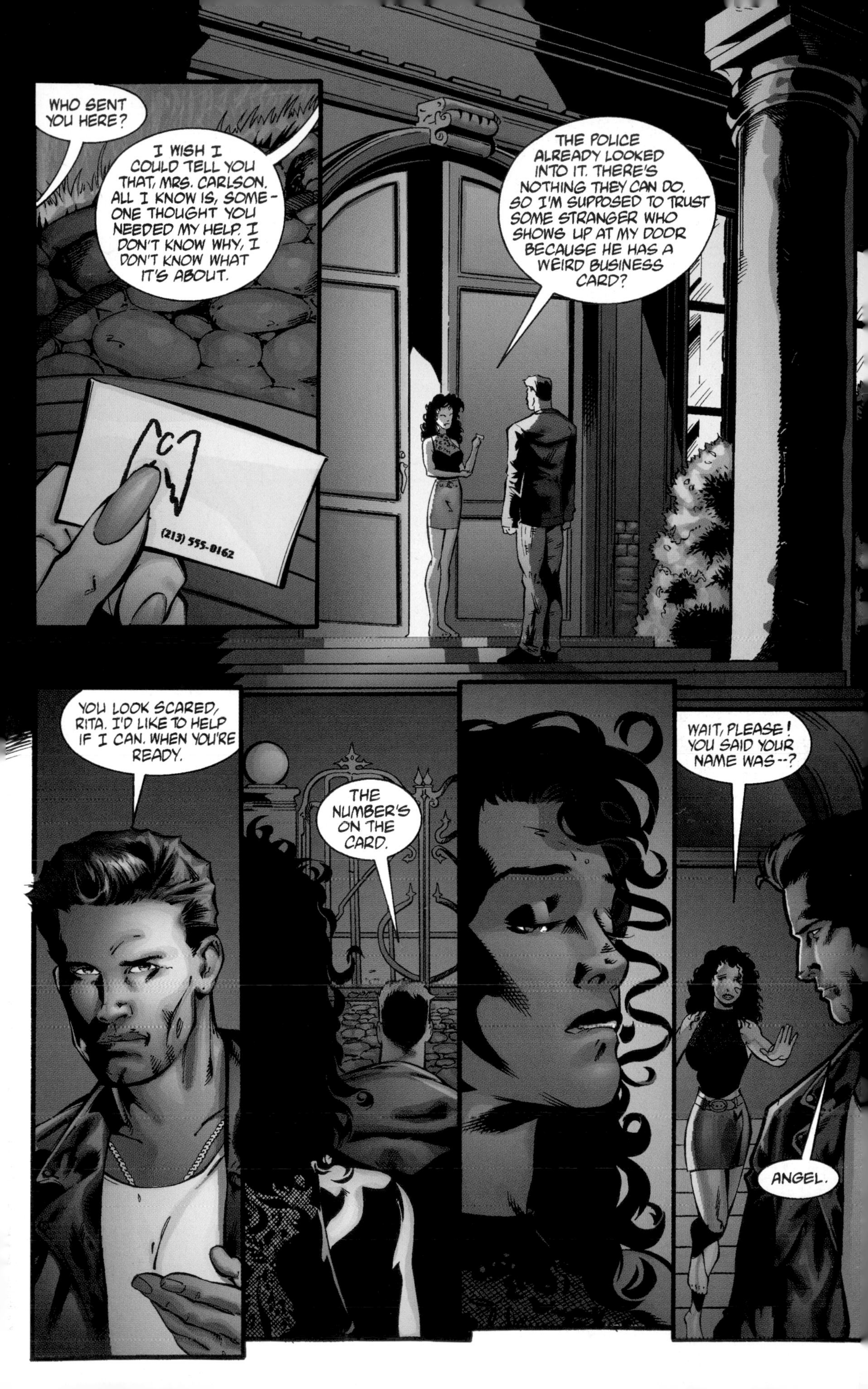
WHO SENT YOU HERE?
I WISH I COULD TELL YOU THAT, MRS. CARLSON. ALL I KNOW IS, SOME-ONE THOUGHT YOU NEEDED MY HELP. I DON'T KNOW WHY, I DON'T KNOW WHAT IT'S ABOUT.
(213) 555-0162
THE POLICE ALREADY LOOKED INTO IT. THERE'S NOTHING THEY CAN DO. SO I'M SUPPOSED TO TRUST SOME STRANGER WHO SHOWS UP AT MY DOOR BECAUSE HE HAS A WEIRD BUSINESS CARD?
YOU LOOK SCARED, RITA. I'D LIKE TO HELP IF I CAN. WHEN YOU'RE READY.
THE NUMBER'S ON THE CARD.
WAIT, PLEASE! YOU SAID YOUR NAME WAS--?
ANGEL.

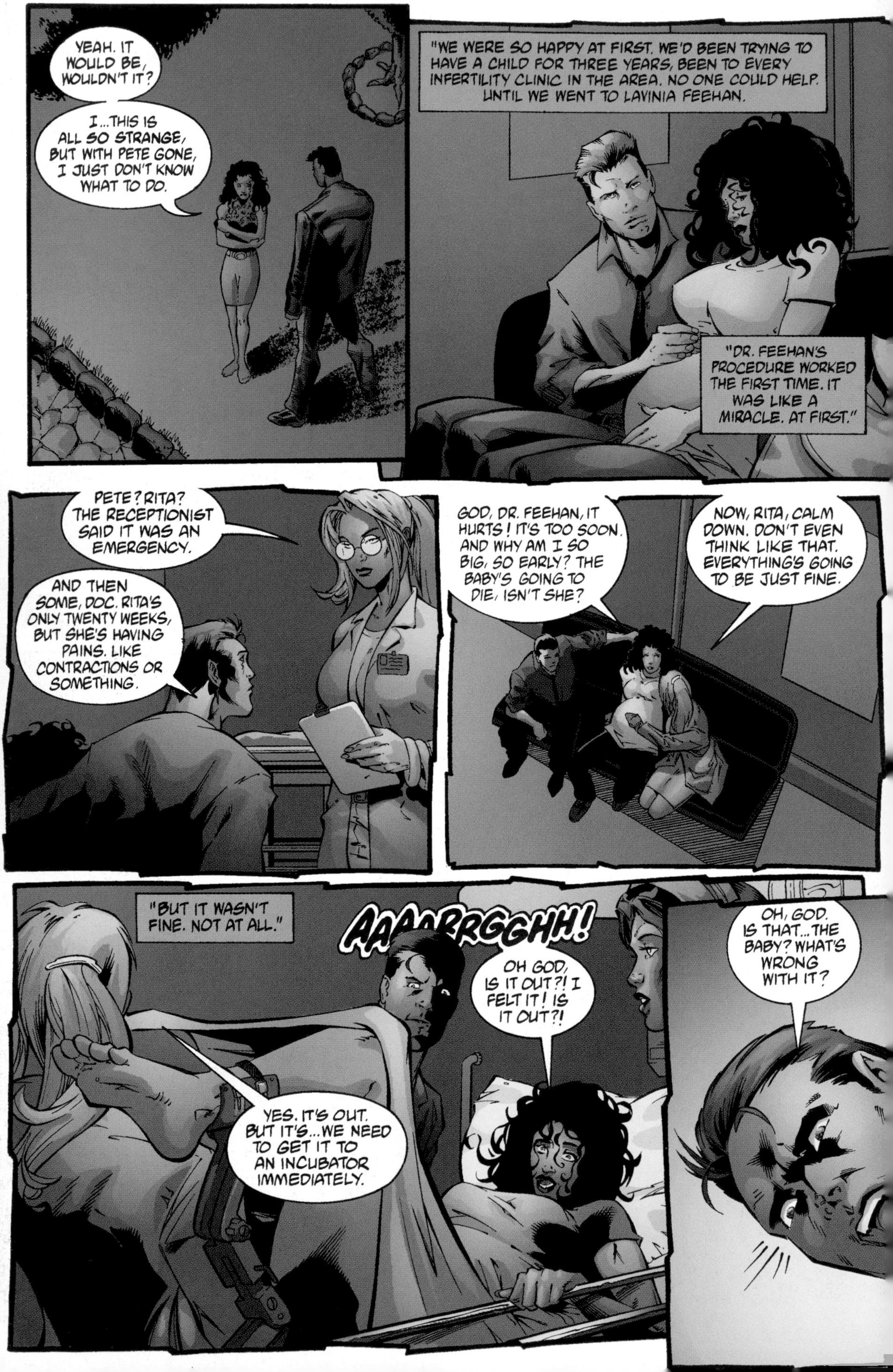
YEAH. IT WOULD BE, WOULDN'T IT?
I...THIS IS ALL SO STRANGE, BUT WITH PETE GONE, I JUST DON'T KNOW WHAT TO DO.
"WE WERE SO HAPPY AT FIRST. WE'D BEEN TRYING TO HAVE A CHILD FOR THREE YEARS, BEEN TO EVERY INFERTILITY CLINIC IN THE AREA. NO ONE COULD HELP. UNTIL WE WENT TO LAVINIA FEEHAN.
"DR. FEEHAN'S PROCEDURE WORKED THE FIRST TIME. IT WAS LIKE A MIRACLE. AT FIRST."
PETE? RITA? THE RECEPTIONIST SAID IT WAS AN EMERGENCY.
AND THEN SOME, DOC. RITA'S ONLY TWENTY WEEKS, BUT SHE'S HAVING PAINS. LIKE CONTRACTIONS OR SOMETHING.
GOD, DR. FEEHAN, IT HURTS! IT'S TOO SOON. AND WHY AM I SO BIG, SO EARLY? THE BABY'S GOING TO DIE, ISN'T SHE?
NOW, RITA, CALM DOWN. DON'T EVEN THINK LIKE THAT. EVERYTHING'S GOING TO BE JUST FINE.
"BUT IT WASN'T FINE. NOT AT ALL."
AAAARRGGHH!
OH GOD, IS IT OUT?! I FELT IT! IS IT OUT?!
YES. IT'S OUT. BUT IT'S...WE NEED TO GET IT TO AN INCUBATOR IMMEDIATELY.
OH, GOD. IS THAT...THE BABY? WHAT'S WRONG WITH IT?

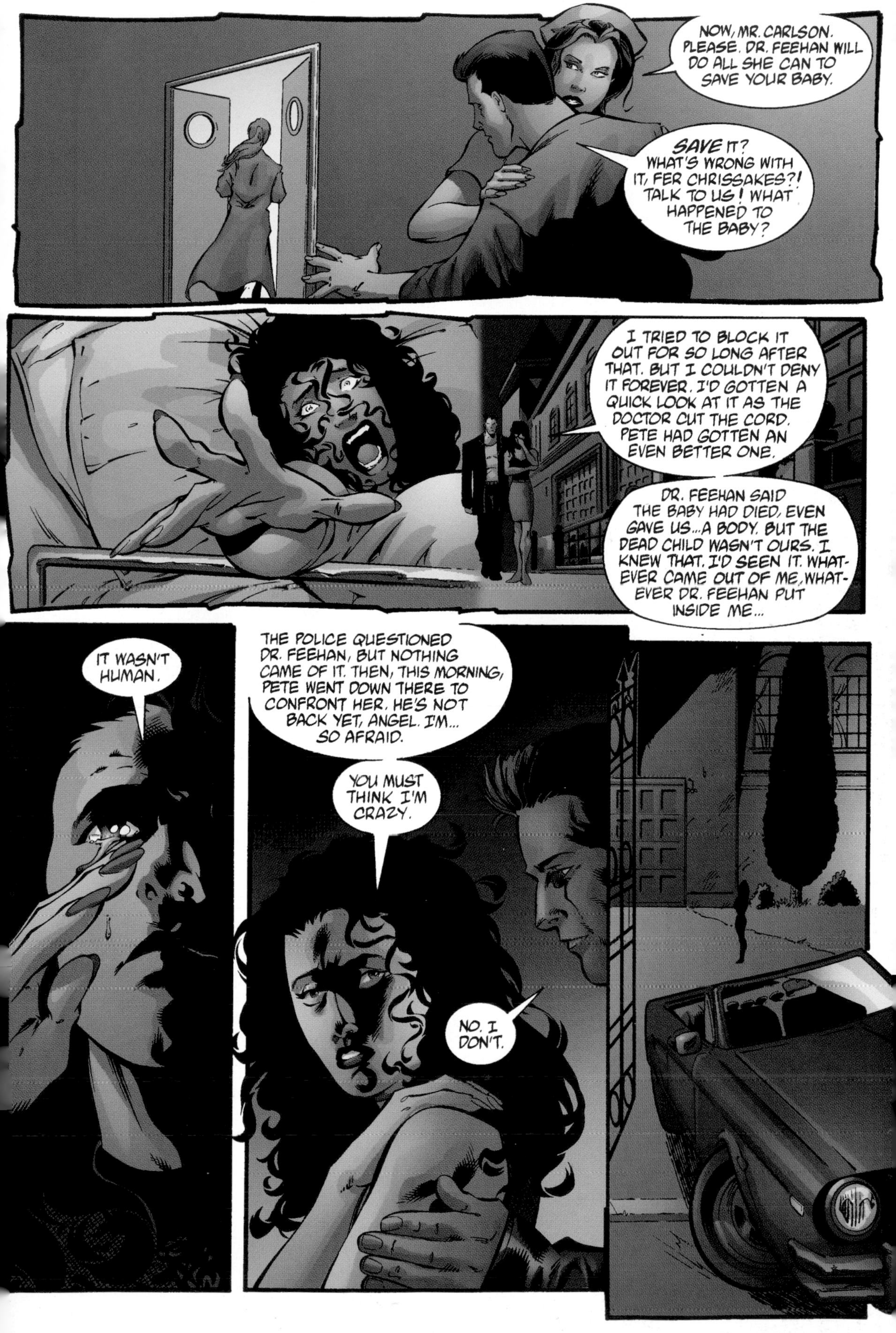
NOW, MR. CARLSON. PLEASE. DR. FEEHAN WILL DO ALL SHE CAN TO SAVE YOUR BABY.
SAVE IT? WHAT'S WRONG WITH IT, FER CHRISSAKES?! TALK TO US! WHAT HAPPENED TO THE BABY?
I TRIED TO BLOCK IT OUT FOR SO LONG AFTER THAT. BUT I COULDN'T DENY IT FOREVER. I'D GOTTEN A QUICK LOOK AT IT AS THE DOCTOR CUT THE CORD. PETE HAD GOTTEN AN EVEN BETTER ONE.
DR. FEEHAN SAID THE BABY HAD DIED, EVEN GAVE US...A BODY. BUT THE DEAD CHILD WASN'T OURS. I KNEW THAT. I'D SEEN IT. WHATEVER CAME OUT OF ME, WHATEVER DR. FEEHAN PUT INSIDE ME...
IT WASN'T HUMAN.
THE POLICE QUESTIONED DR. FEEHAN, BUT NOTHING CAME OF IT. THEN, THIS MORNING, PETE WENT DOWN THERE TO CONFRONT HER. HE'S NOT BACK YET, ANGEL. I'M... SO AFRAID.
YOU MUST THINK I'M CRAZY.
NO. I DON'T.

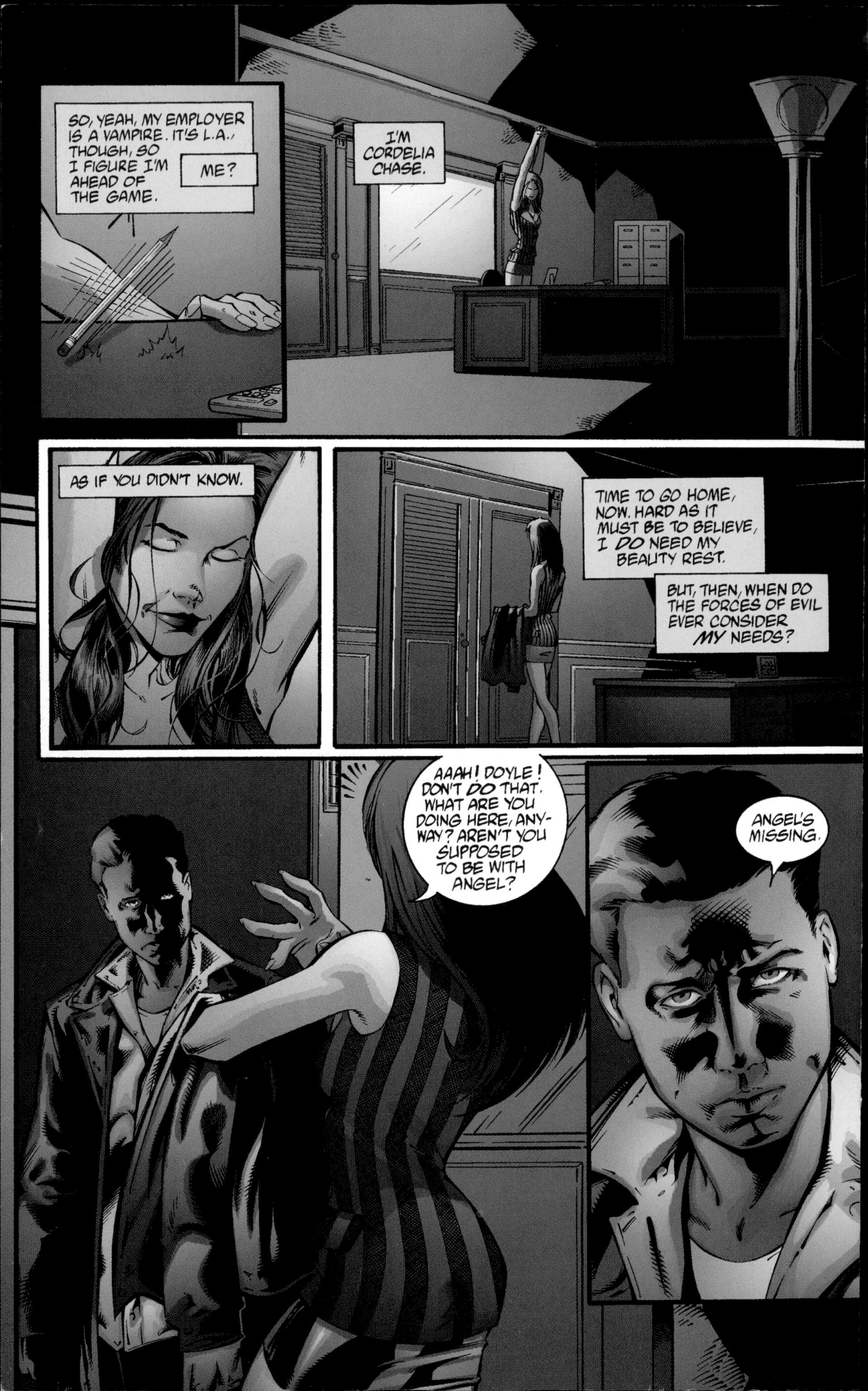
SO, YEAH, MY EMPLOYER IS A VAMPIRE. IT'S L.A., THOUGH, SO I FIGURE I'M AHEAD OF THE GAME.
ME?
I'M CORDELIA CHASE.
AS IF YOU DIDN'T KNOW.
TIME TO GO HOME, NOW. HARD AS IT MUST BE TO BELIEVE, I DO NEED MY BEAUTY REST.
BUT, THEN, WHEN DO THE FORCES OF EVIL EVER CONSIDER MY NEEDS?
AAAH! DOYLE! DON'T DO THAT. WHAT ARE YOU DOING HERE, ANY-WAY? AREN'T YOU SUPPOSED TO BE WITH ANGEL?
ANGEL'S MISSING.

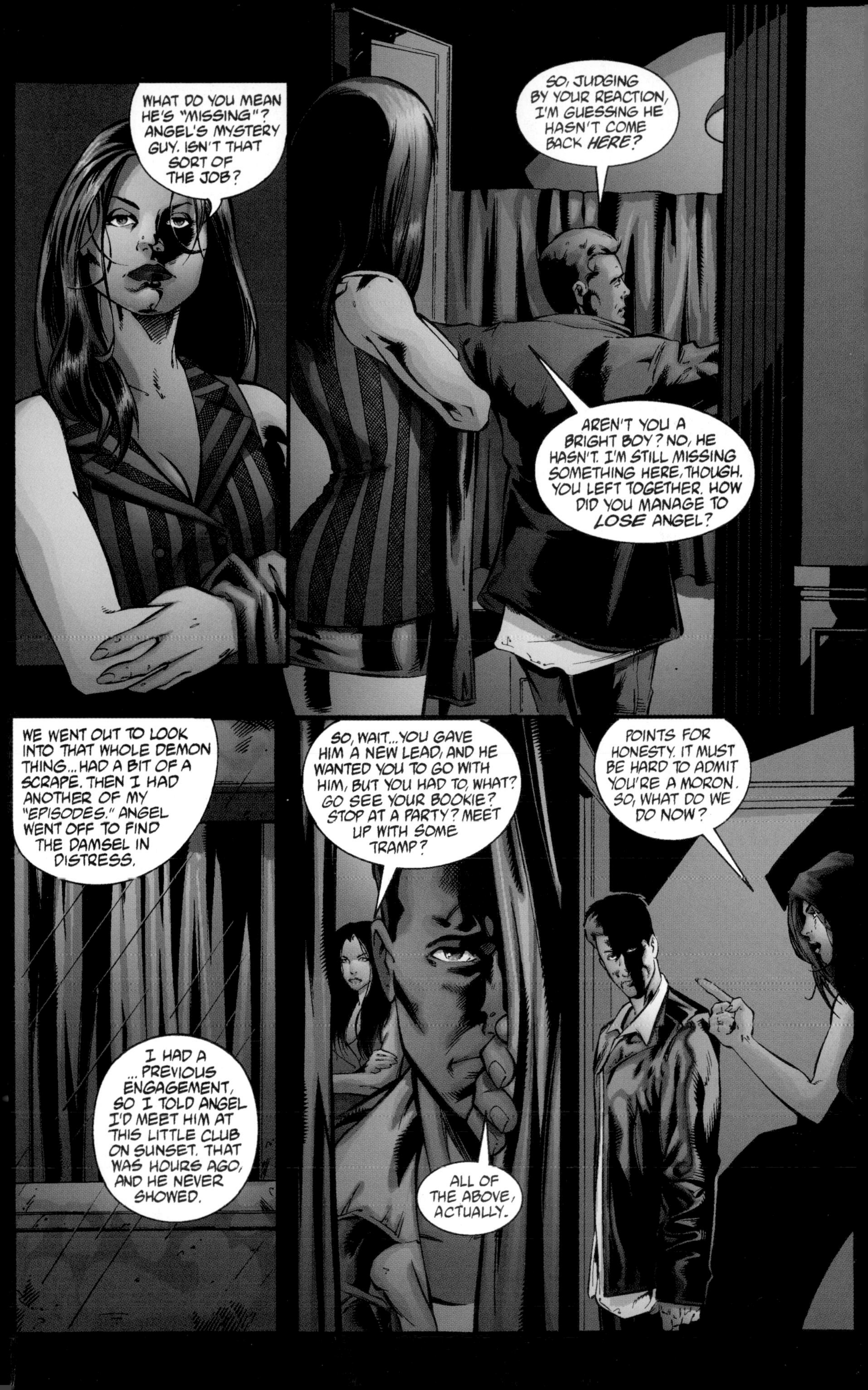
WHAT DO YOU MEAN HE'S "MISSING"? ANGEL'S MYSTERY GUY. ISN'T THAT SORT OF THE JOB?
SO, JUDGING BY YOUR REACTION, I'M GUESSING HE HASN'T COME BACK *HERE*?
AREN'T YOU A BRIGHT BOY? NO, HE HASN'T. I'M STILL MISSING SOMETHING HERE, THOUGH. YOU LEFT TOGETHER. HOW DID YOU MANAGE TO *LOSE* ANGEL?
WE WENT OUT TO LOOK INTO THAT WHOLE DEMON THING... HAD A BIT OF A SCRAPE. THEN I HAD ANOTHER OF MY "EPISODES." ANGEL WENT OFF TO FIND THE DAMSEL IN DISTRESS.
I HAD A ... PREVIOUS ENGAGEMENT, SO I TOLD ANGEL I'D MEET HIM AT THIS LITTLE CLUB ON SUNSET. THAT WAS HOURS AGO, AND HE NEVER SHOWED.
SO, WAIT... YOU GAVE HIM A NEW LEAD, AND HE WANTED YOU TO GO WITH HIM, BUT YOU HAD TO, WHAT? GO SEE YOUR BOOKIE? STOP AT A PARTY? MEET UP WITH SOME TRAMP?
ALL OF THE ABOVE, ACTUALLY.
POINTS FOR HONESTY. IT MUST BE HARD TO ADMIT YOU'RE A MORON. SO, WHAT DO WE DO NOW?

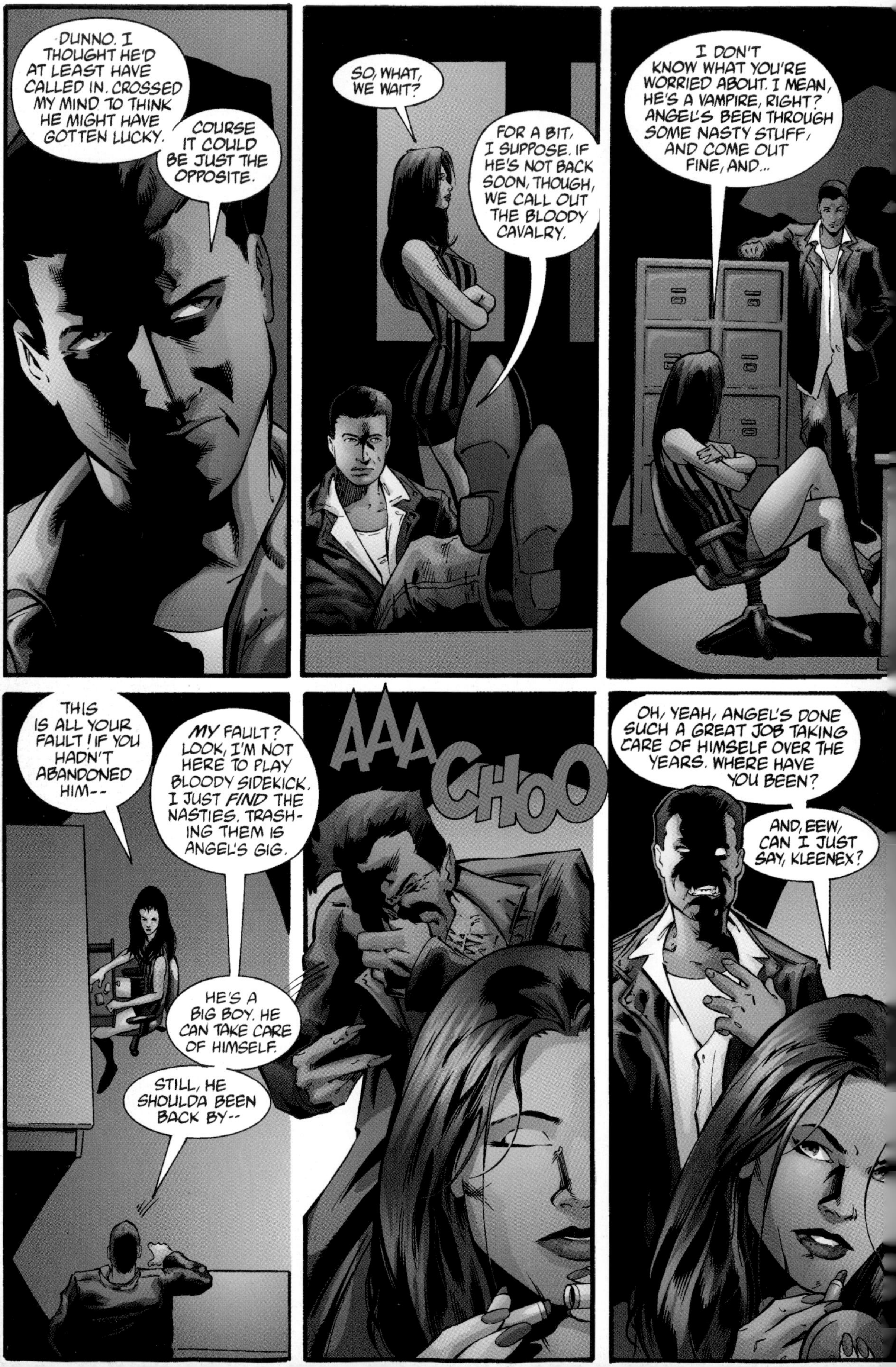
DUNNO. I THOUGHT HE'D AT LEAST HAVE CALLED IN. CROSSED MY MIND TO THINK HE MIGHT HAVE GOTTEN LUCKY.
COURSE IT COULD BE JUST THE OPPOSITE.
SO, WHAT, WE WAIT?
FOR A BIT, I SUPPOSE. IF HE'S NOT BACK SOON, THOUGH, WE CALL OUT THE BLOODY CAVALRY.
I DON'T KNOW WHAT YOU'RE WORRIED ABOUT. I MEAN, HE'S A VAMPIRE, RIGHT? ANGEL'S BEEN THROUGH SOME NASTY STUFF, AND COME OUT FINE, AND...
THIS IS ALL YOUR FAULT! IF YOU HADN'T ABANDONED HIM--
MY FAULT? LOOK, I'M NOT HERE TO PLAY BLOODY SIDEKICK. I JUST FIND THE NASTIES. TRASH-ING THEM IS ANGEL'S GIG.
HE'S A BIG BOY. HE CAN TAKE CARE OF HIMSELF.
STILL, HE SHOULDA BEEN BACK BY--
AAACHOO
OH, YEAH, ANGEL'S DONE SUCH A GREAT JOB TAKING CARE OF HIMSELF OVER THE YEARS. WHERE HAVE YOU BEEN?
AND, EEW, CAN I JUST SAY, KLEENEX?

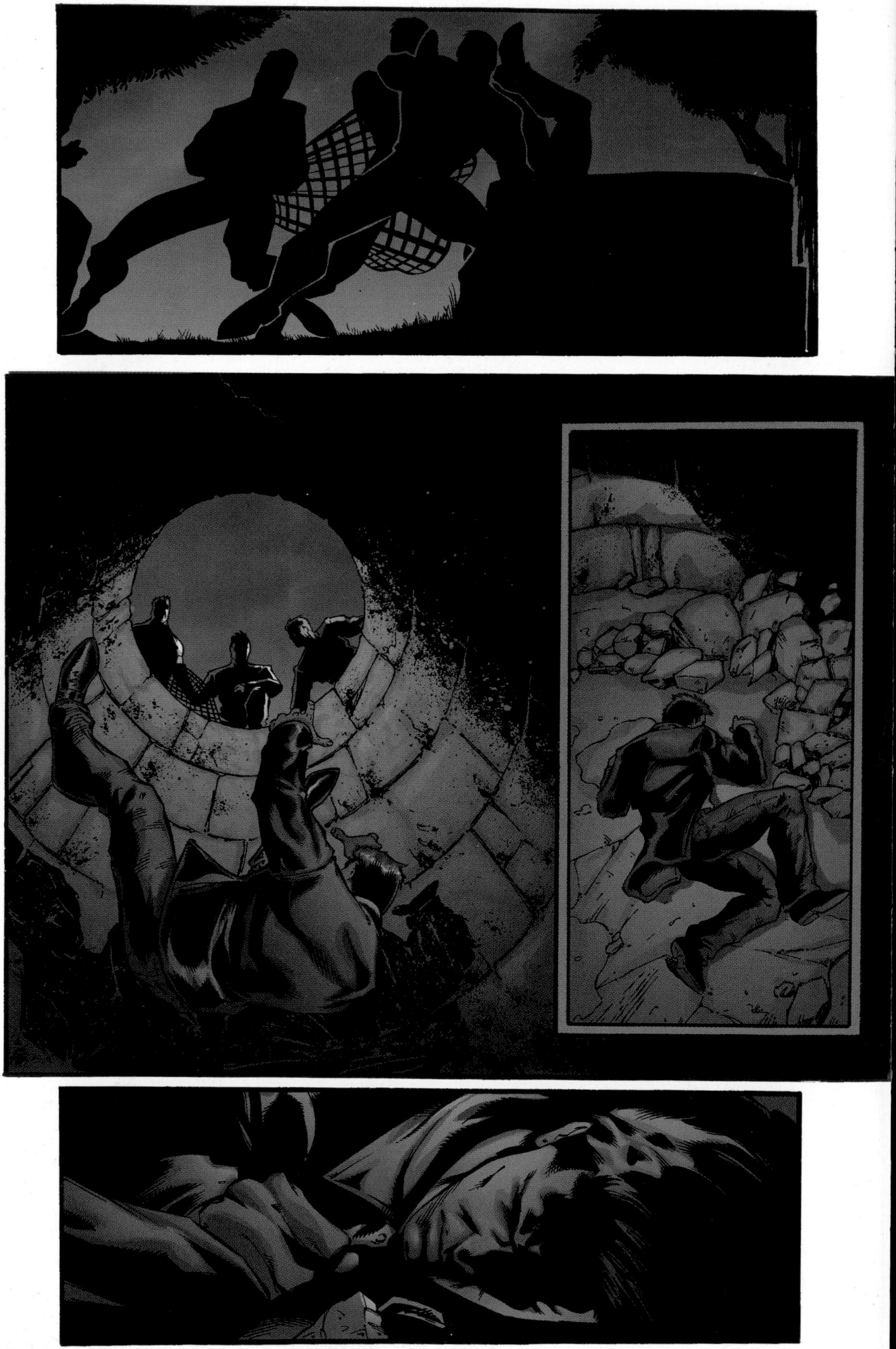

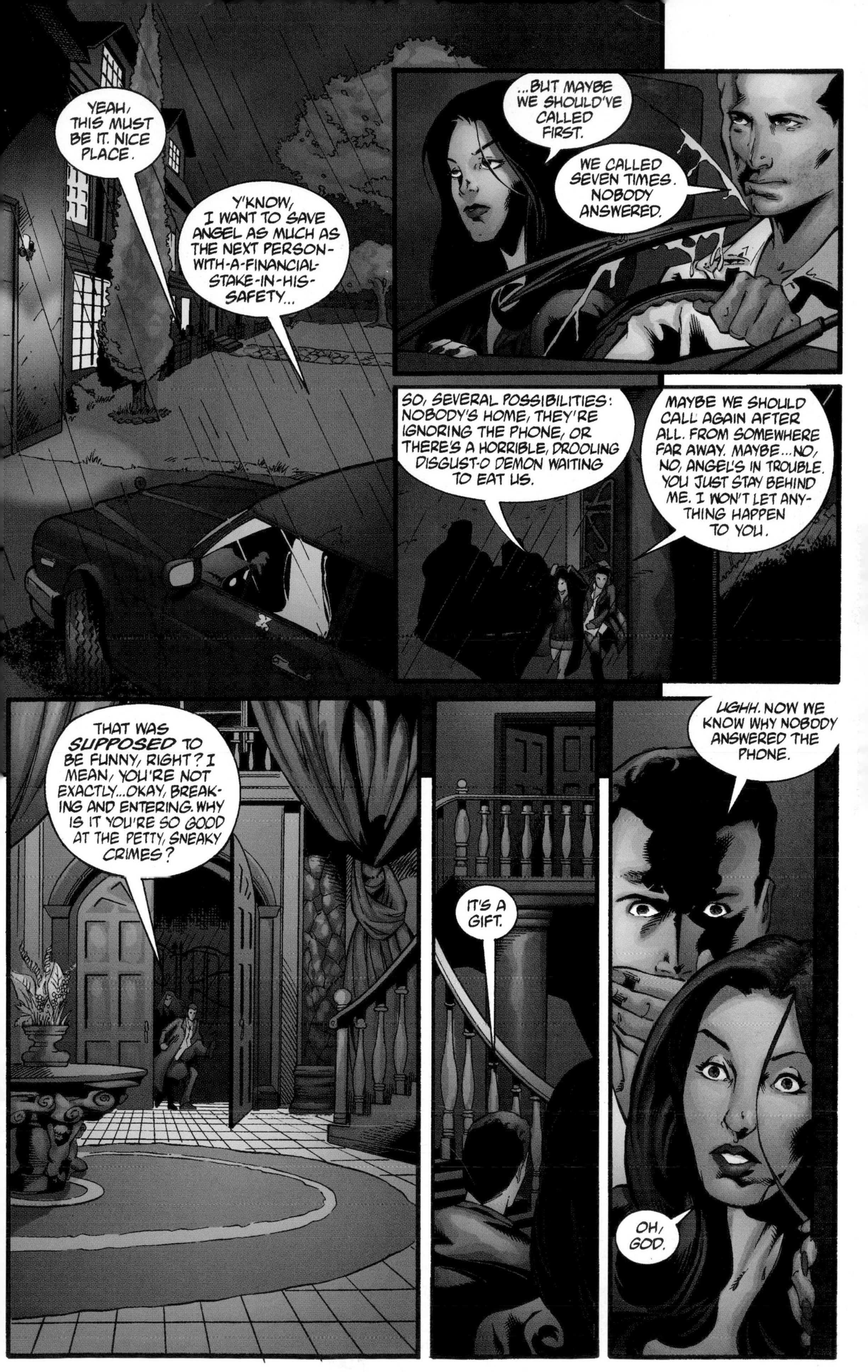
YEAH, THIS MUST BE IT. NICE PLACE.
Y'KNOW, I WANT TO SAVE ANGEL AS MUCH AS THE NEXT PERSON-WITH-A-FINANCIAL-STAKE-IN-HIS-SAFETY...
...BUT MAYBE WE SHOULD'VE CALLED FIRST.
WE CALLED SEVEN TIMES. NOBODY ANSWERED.
SO, SEVERAL POSSIBILITIES: NOBODY'S HOME, THEY'RE IGNORING THE PHONE, OR THERE'S A HORRIBLE, DROOLING DISGUST-O DEMON WAITING TO EAT US.
MAYBE WE SHOULD CALL AGAIN AFTER ALL. FROM SOMEWHERE FAR AWAY. MAYBE...NO, NO, ANGEL'S IN TROUBLE. YOU JUST STAY BEHIND ME. I WON'T LET ANYTHING HAPPEN TO YOU.
THAT WAS *SUPPOSED* TO BE FUNNY, RIGHT? I MEAN, YOU'RE NOT EXACTLY...OKAY, BREAKING AND ENTERING. WHY IS IT YOU'RE SO GOOD AT THE PETTY, SNEAKY CRIMES?
IT'S A GIFT.
UGHH. NOW WE KNOW WHY NOBODY ANSWERED THE PHONE.
OH, GOD.

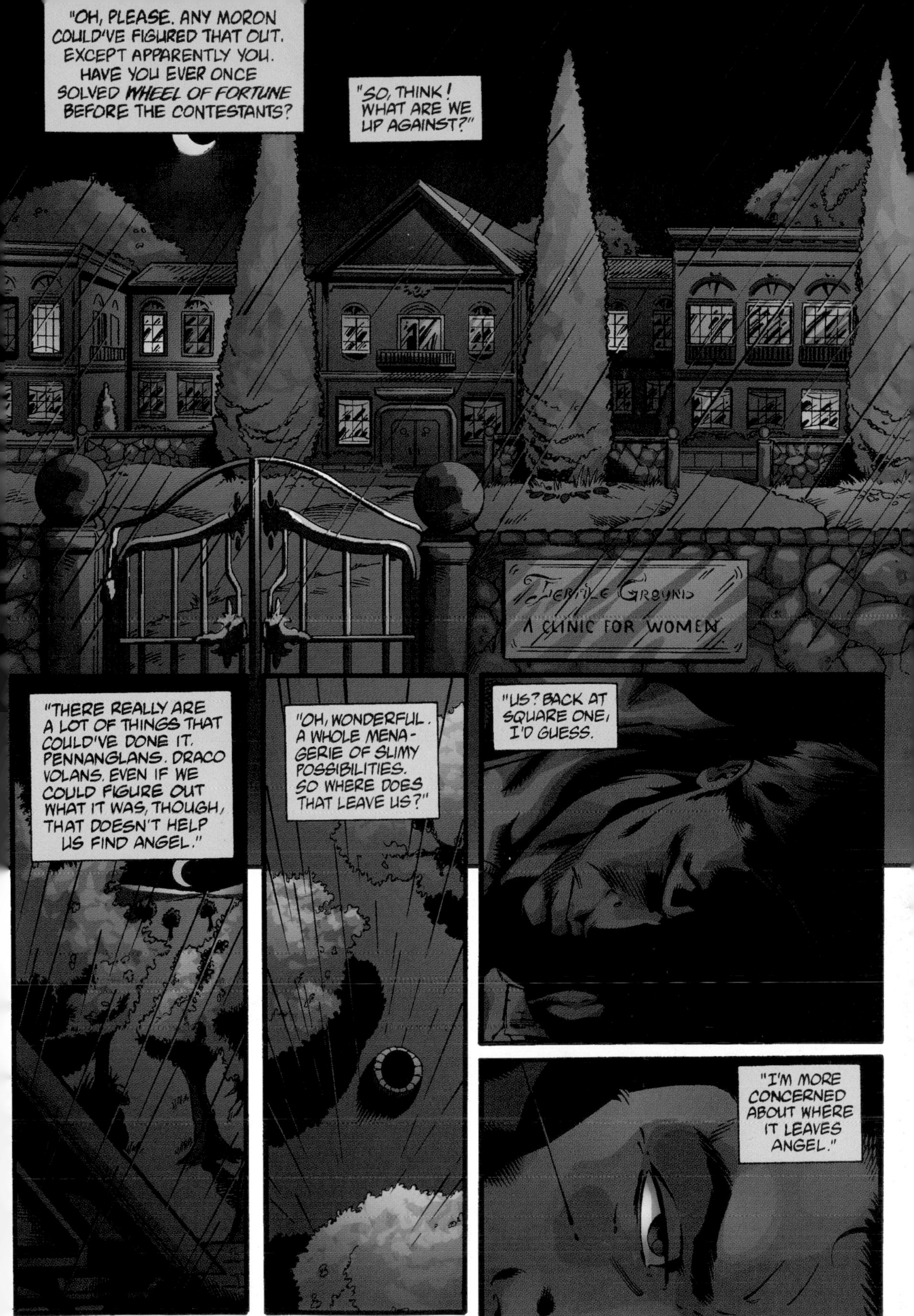
"OH, PLEASE. ANY MORON COULD'VE FIGURED THAT OUT. EXCEPT APPARENTLY YOU. HAVE YOU EVER ONCE SOLVED *WHEEL OF FORTUNE* BEFORE THE CONTESTANTS?
"SO, THINK! WHAT ARE WE UP AGAINST?"
FERTILE GROUND
A CLINIC FOR WOMEN
"THERE REALLY ARE A LOT OF THINGS THAT COULD'VE DONE IT. PENNANGLANS. DRACO VOLANS. EVEN IF WE COULD FIGURE OUT WHAT IT WAS, THOUGH, THAT DOESN'T HELP US FIND ANGEL."
"OH, WONDERFUL. A WHOLE MENAGERIE OF SLIMY POSSIBILITIES. SO WHERE DOES THAT LEAVE US?"
"US? BACK AT SQUARE ONE, I'D GUESS.
"I'M MORE CONCERNED ABOUT WHERE IT LEAVES ANGEL."

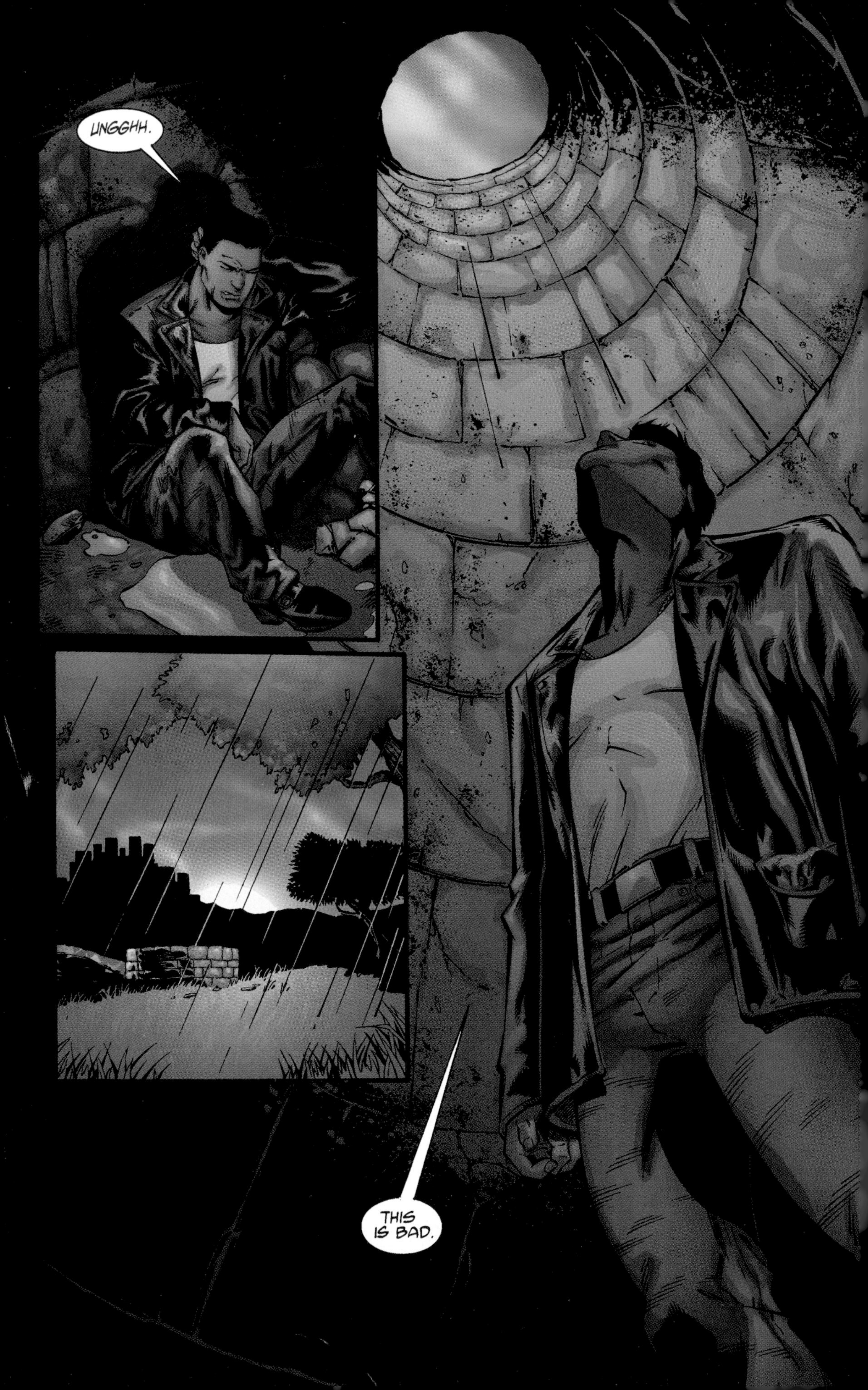
UNGGHH.
THIS IS BAD.

Cover by JEFF MATSUDA and JON SIBAL
Colors by GUY MAJOR

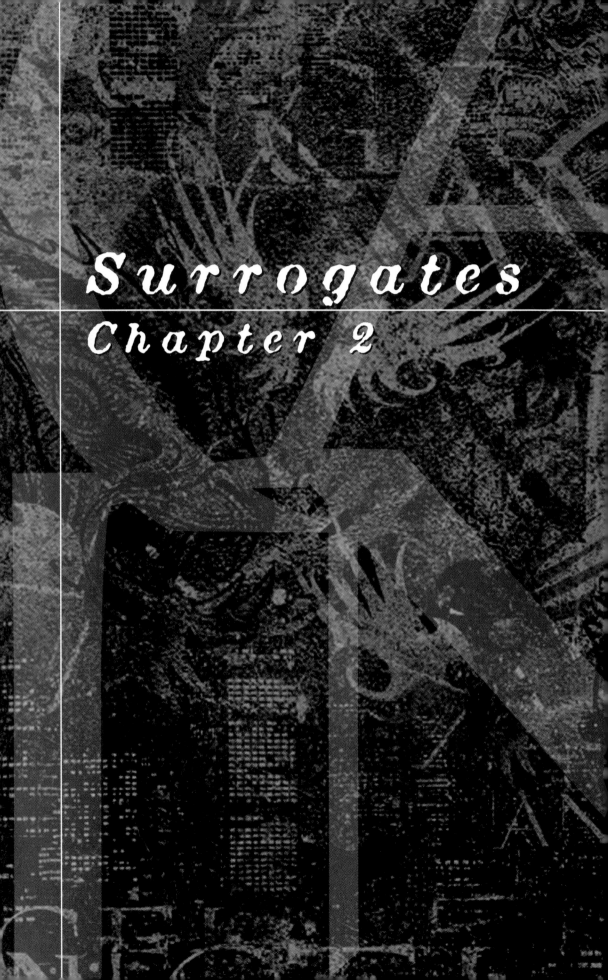

Surrogates
Chapter 2

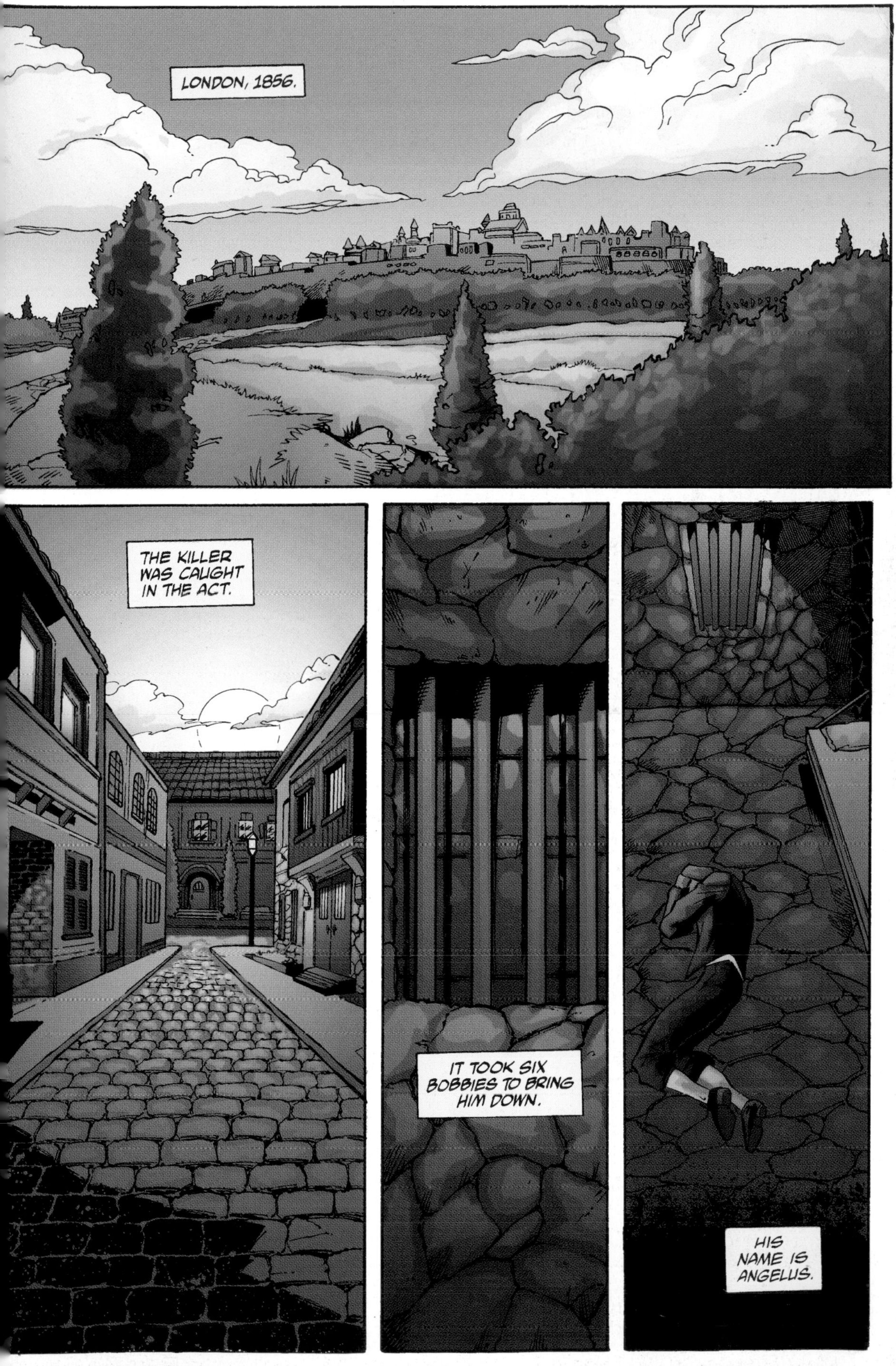
LONDON, 1856.
THE KILLER WAS CAUGHT IN THE ACT.
IT TOOK SIX BOBBIES TO BRING HIM DOWN.
HIS NAME IS ANGELUS.

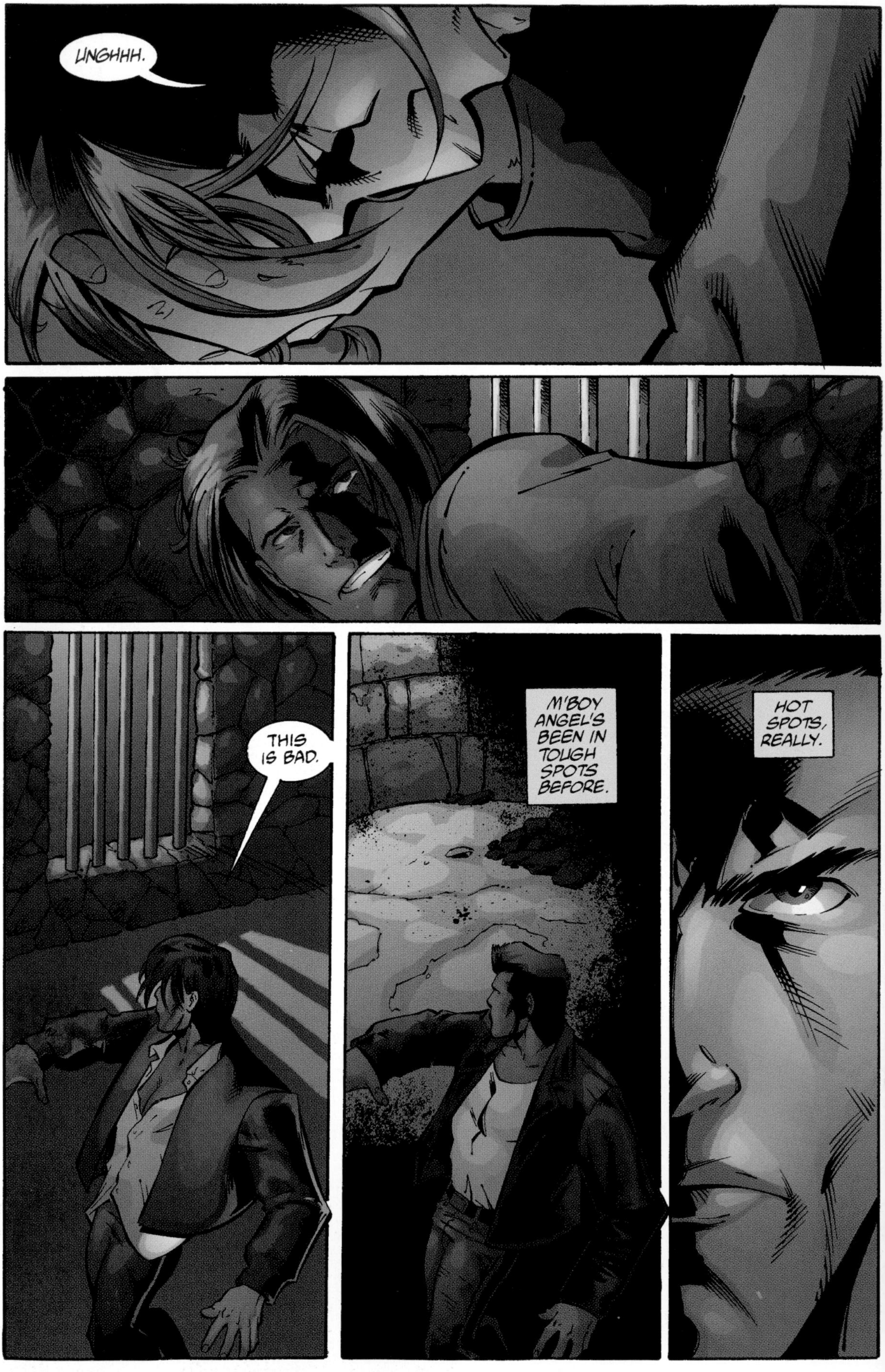
UNGHHH.
THIS IS BAD.
M'BOY ANGEL'S BEEN IN TOUGH SPOTS BEFORE.
HOT SPOTS, REALLY.

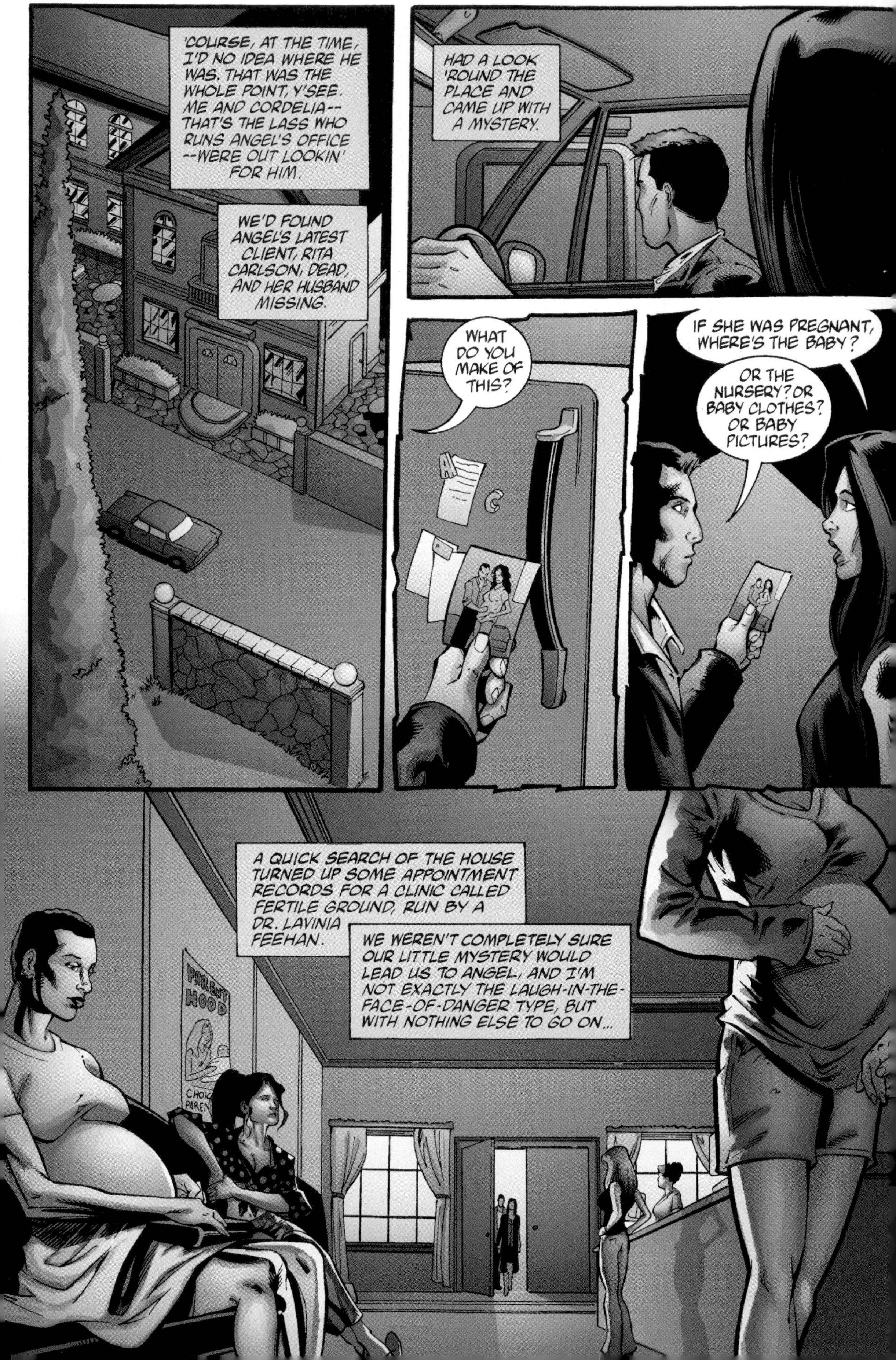
'COURSE, AT THE TIME, I'D NO IDEA WHERE HE WAS. THAT WAS THE WHOLE POINT, Y'SEE. ME AND CORDELIA-- THAT'S THE LASS WHO RUNS ANGEL'S OFFICE --WERE OUT LOOKIN' FOR HIM.
WE'D FOUND ANGEL'S LATEST CLIENT, RITA CARLSON, DEAD, AND HER HUSBAND MISSING.
HAD A LOOK 'ROUND THE PLACE AND CAME UP WITH A MYSTERY.
WHAT DO YOU MAKE OF THIS?
IF SHE WAS PREGNANT, WHERE'S THE BABY?
OR THE NURSERY? OR BABY CLOTHES? OR BABY PICTURES?
A QUICK SEARCH OF THE HOUSE TURNED UP SOME APPOINTMENT RECORDS FOR A CLINIC CALLED FERTILE GROUND, RUN BY A DR. LAVINIA FEEHAN.
WE WEREN'T COMPLETELY SURE OUR LITTLE MYSTERY WOULD LEAD US TO ANGEL, AND I'M NOT EXACTLY THE LAUGH-IN-THE-FACE-OF-DANGER TYPE, BUT WITH NOTHING ELSE TO GO ON...
PARENT HOOD

DR. FEEHAN. THANKS SO MUCH FOR TAKING THE TIME.

WE'RE AT THE END OF OUR ROPE, DOC. IT ISN'T THAT I DON'T LIKE THE PRACTICE, BUT--

YES, SO YOU MENTIONED. SO TRAGIC, BUT NOT ALL THAT SURPRISING.

RITA MANAGED TO CONCEIVE, BUT THE BABY WAS PREMATURE, AND STILLBORN. STILL, THEY WERE AN ISOLATED CASE. OUR SUCCESS RATES ARE--

NOT AT ALL, MR....DWYER, WAS IT? WHAT CAN I DO FOR YOU?

WE WERE TRYING TO HAVE A CHILD FOR ALMOST TWO YEARS. PETER AND RITA CARLSON TOLD US YOU WERE THE BEST. OF COURSE, THAT WAS BEFORE... WHAT HAPPENED ...WITH THEM.

YEAH. THE BABY. AND THEN WITH PETER--

CALL TO MAKE AN APPOINTMENT FOR NEXT WEEK. WE'LL SEE IF WE CAN'T GET TO THE ROOT OF YOUR PROBLEM.

THANK YOU FOR YOUR TIME.

SHE'S PRETTY DEFENSIVE ABOUT THE CARLSONS. AND A LITTLE CREEPY, BUT THIS IS L.A., RIGHT? WEIRD'S ALWAYS IN STYLE. SHE SEEMS A LITTLE TOO HUMAN TO HAVE KILLED MRS. CARLSON.

PETER CARLSON ISN'T THE FIRST HUSBAND TO ABANDON HIS WIFE AFTER SOMETHING AS TRAUMATIC AS THAT. BUT DON'T WORRY, DEAR. OUR SUCCESS RATE IS VERY HIGH. YOU'RE IN GOOD HANDS HERE.

I'VE GOT KIND OF A SENSE ABOUT THESE THINGS. WHATEVER OUR DR. FEEHAN IS, IT BLOODY WELL ISN'T HUMAN.

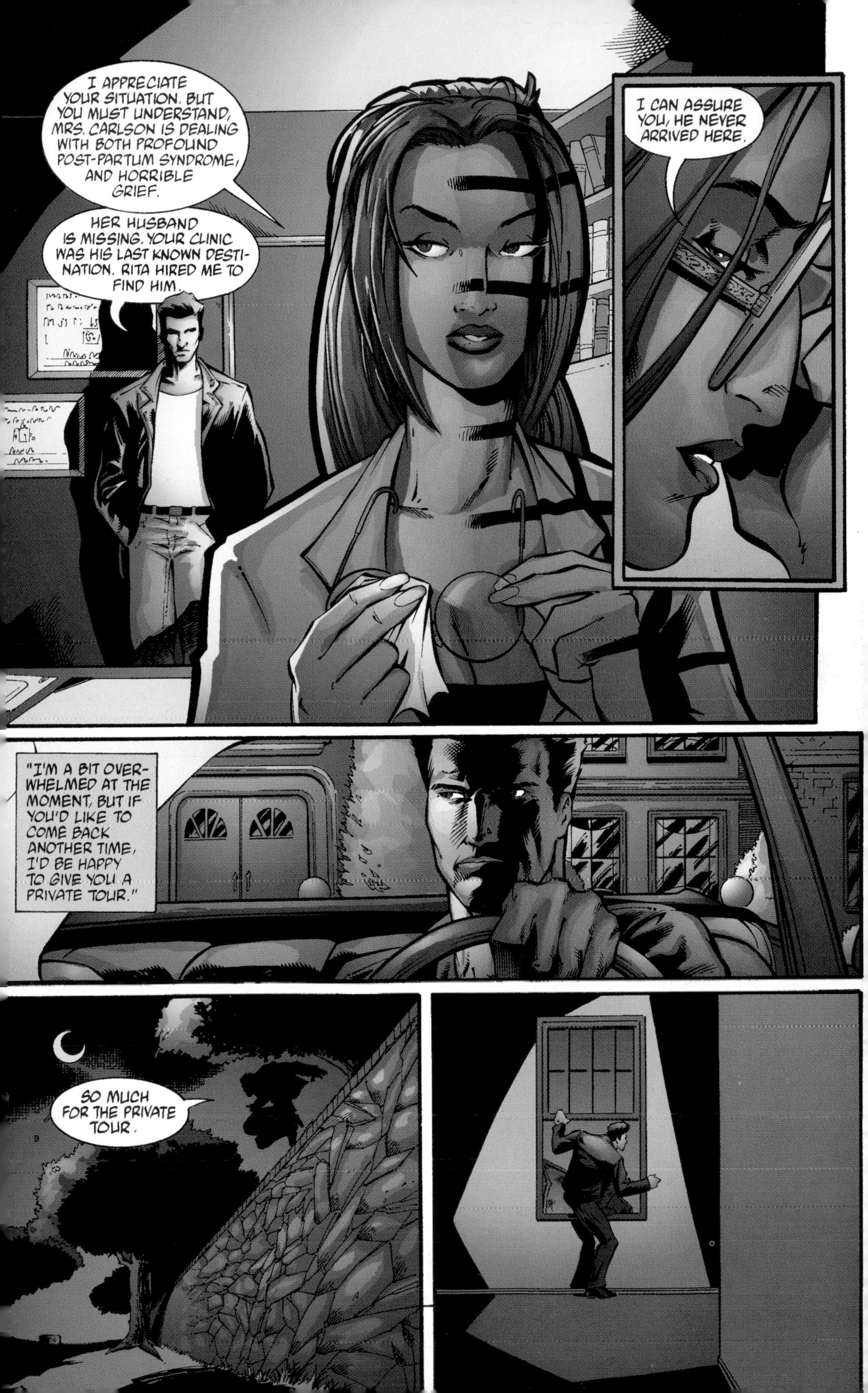
I APPRECIATE YOUR SITUATION. BUT YOU MUST UNDERSTAND, MRS. CARLSON IS DEALING WITH BOTH PROFOUND POST-PARTUM SYNDROME, AND HORRIBLE GRIEF.
HER HUSBAND IS MISSING. YOUR CLINIC WAS HIS LAST KNOWN DESTINATION. RITA HIRED ME TO FIND HIM.
I CAN ASSURE YOU, HE NEVER ARRIVED HERE.
"I'M A BIT OVERWHELMED AT THE MOMENT, BUT IF YOU'D LIKE TO COME BACK ANOTHER TIME, I'D BE HAPPY TO GIVE YOU A PRIVATE TOUR."
SO MUCH FOR THE PRIVATE TOUR.

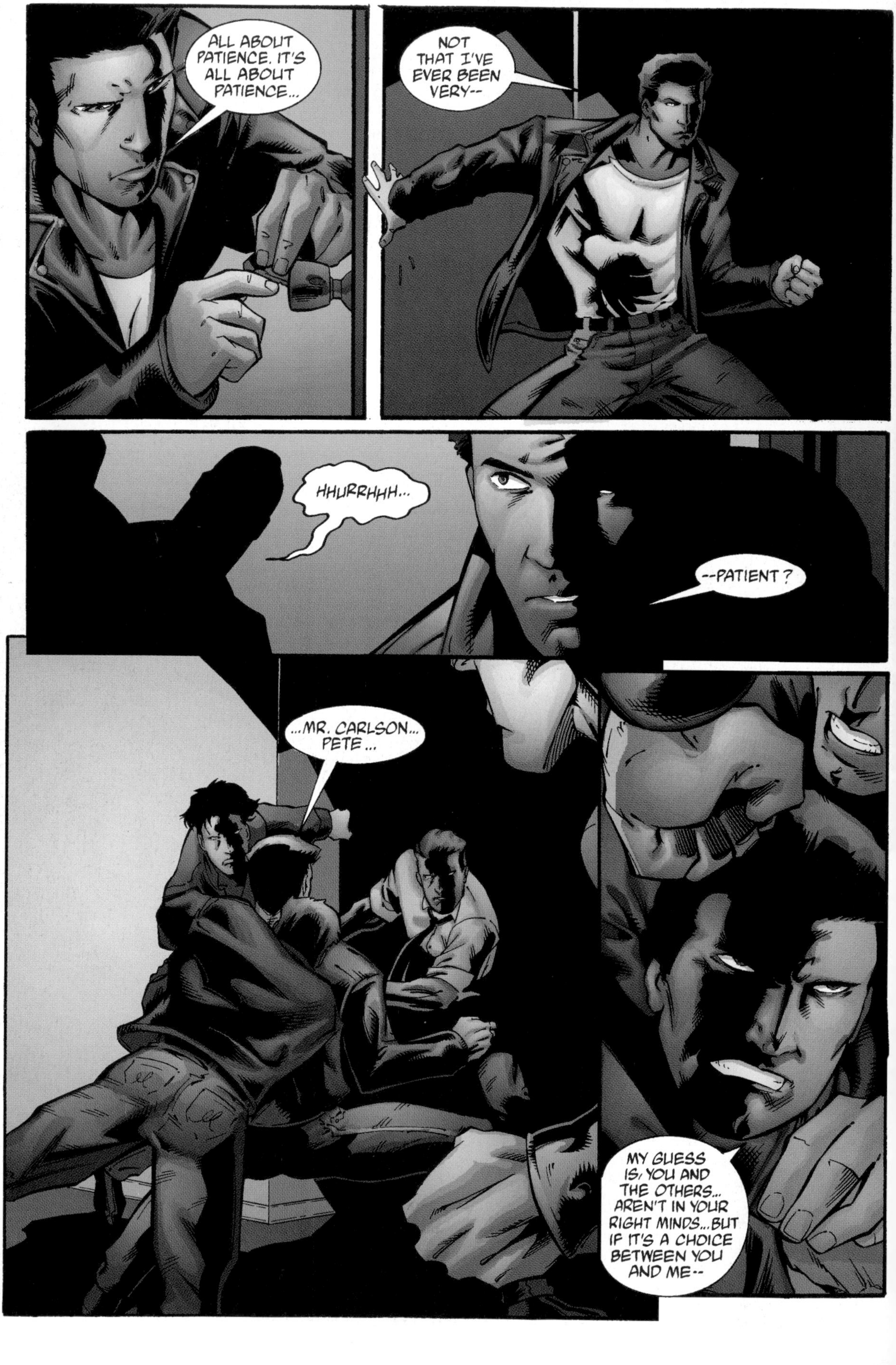

ALL ABOUT PATIENCE. IT'S ALL ABOUT PATIENCE...
NOT THAT I'VE EVER BEEN VERY--
HHURRHHH...
--PATIENT?
...MR. CARLSON... PETE...
MY GUESS IS, YOU AND THE OTHERS... AREN'T IN YOUR RIGHT MINDS...BUT IF IT'S A CHOICE BETWEEN YOU AND ME--

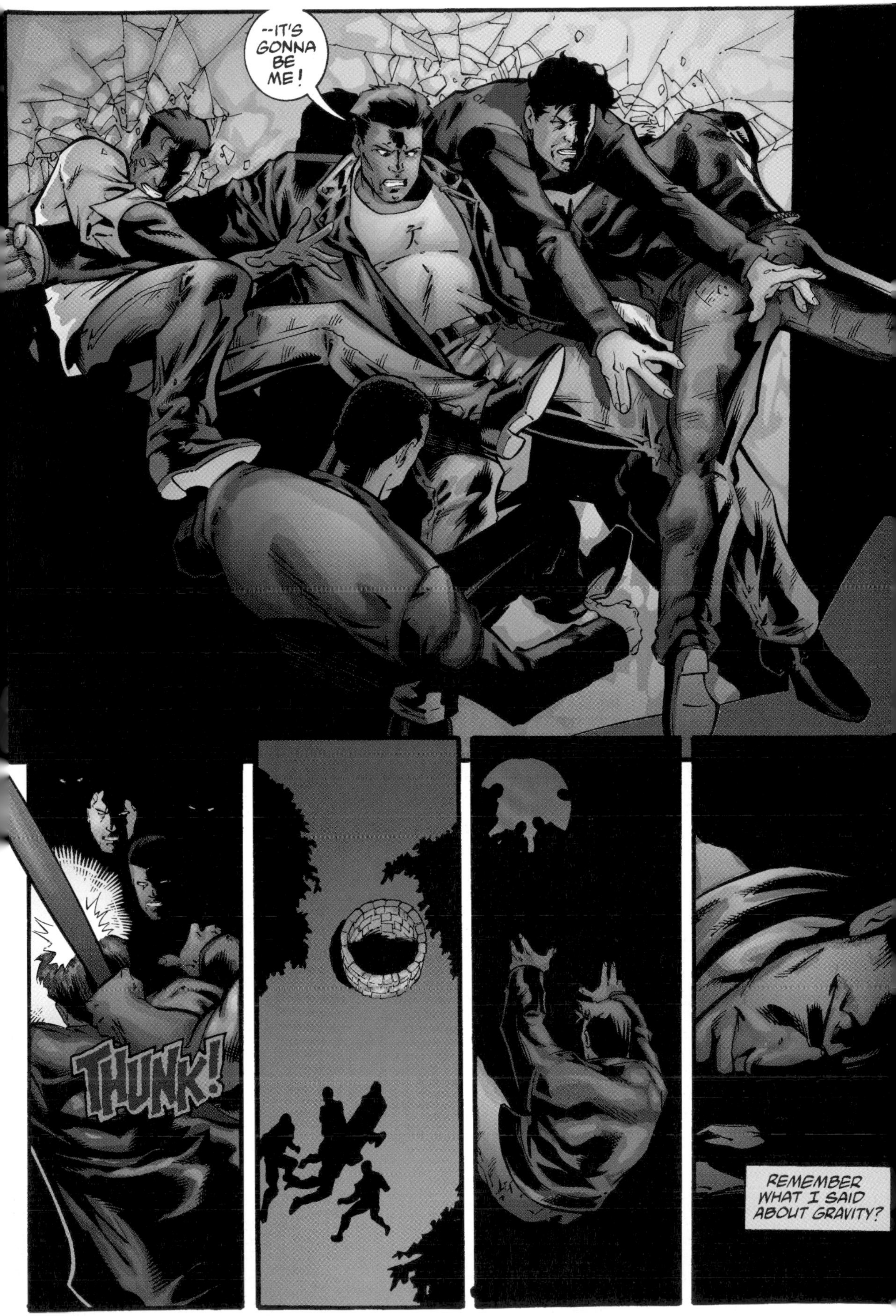
--IT'S GONNA BE ME!
THUNK!
REMEMBER WHAT I SAID ABOUT GRAVITY?

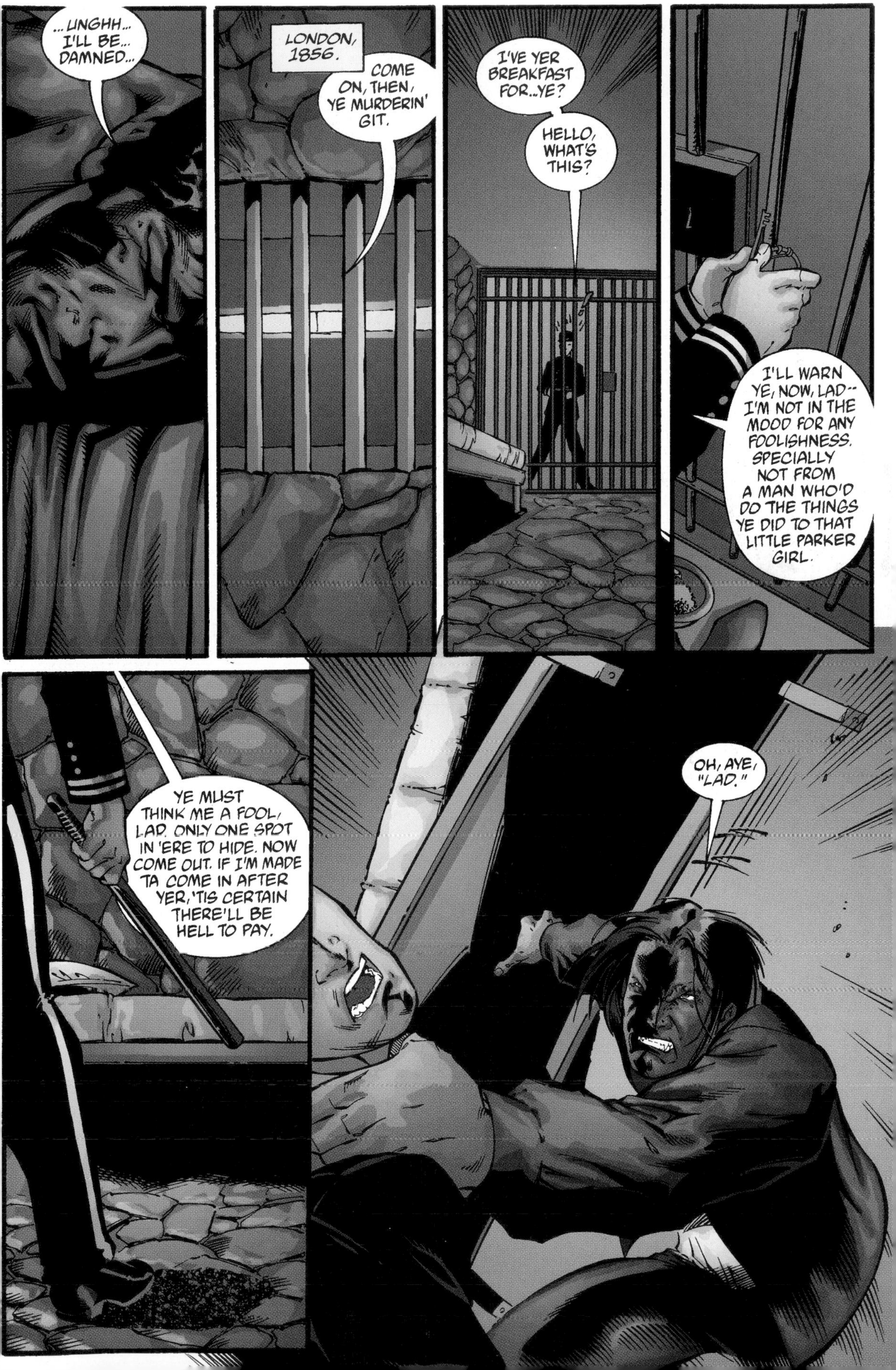
...UNGHH... I'LL BE... DAMNED...
LONDON, 1856.
COME ON, THEN, YE MURDERIN' GIT.
I'VE YER BREAKFAST FOR...YE?
HELLO, WHAT'S THIS?
I'LL WARN YE, NOW, LAD-- I'M NOT IN THE MOOD FOR ANY FOOLISHNESS. SPECIALLY NOT FROM A MAN WHO'D DO THE THINGS YE DID TO THAT LITTLE PARKER GIRL.
YE MUST THINK ME A FOOL, LAD. ONLY ONE SPOT IN 'ERE TO HIDE. NOW COME OUT. IF I'M MADE TA COME IN AFTER YER, 'TIS CERTAIN THERE'LL BE HELL TO PAY.
OH, AYE, "LAD."

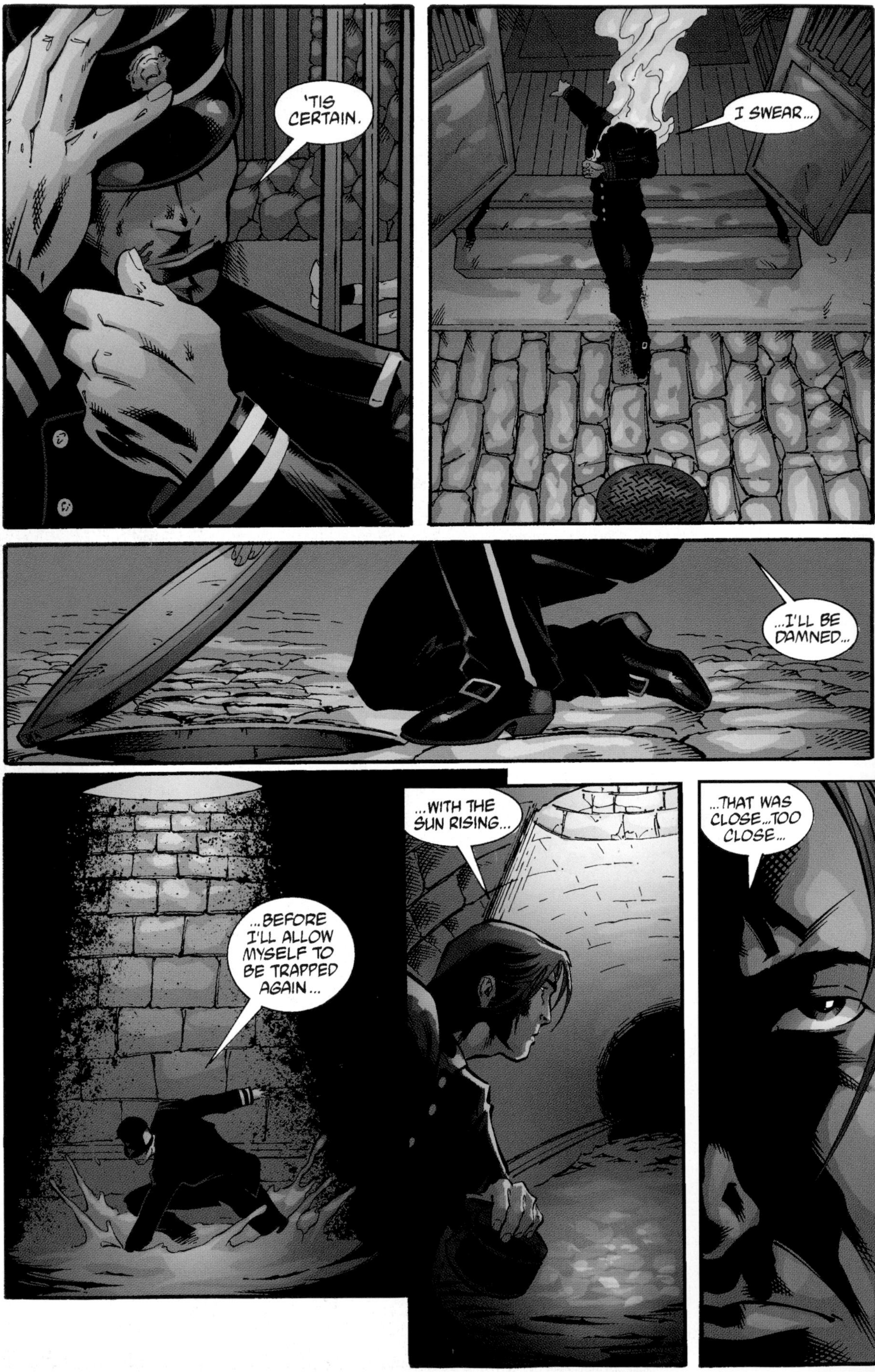
'TIS CERTAIN.
I SWEAR...
...I'LL BE DAMNED...
...BEFORE I'LL ALLOW MYSELF TO BE TRAPPED AGAIN...
...WITH THE SUN RISING...
...THAT WAS CLOSE...TOO CLOSE...

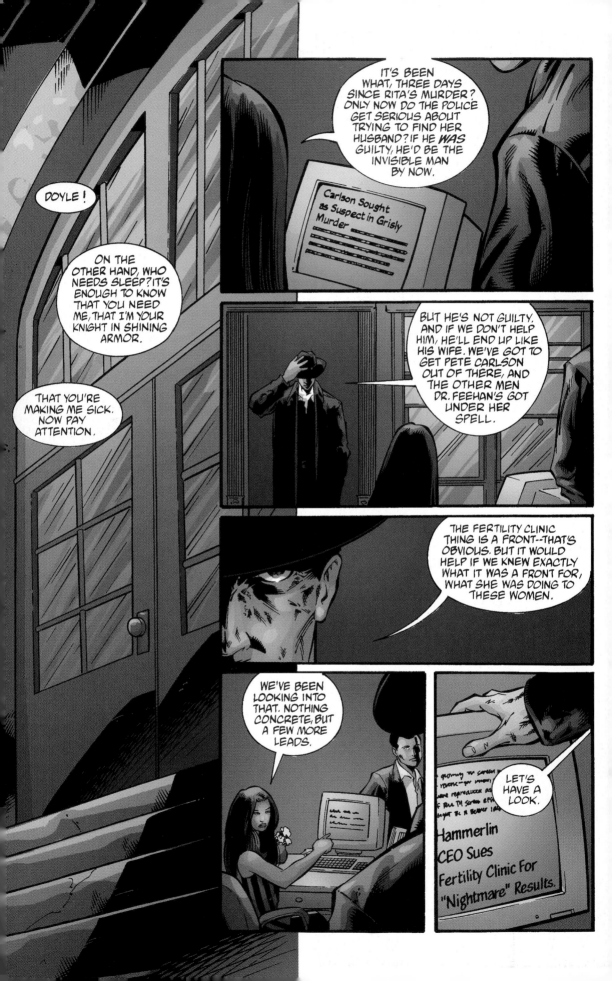

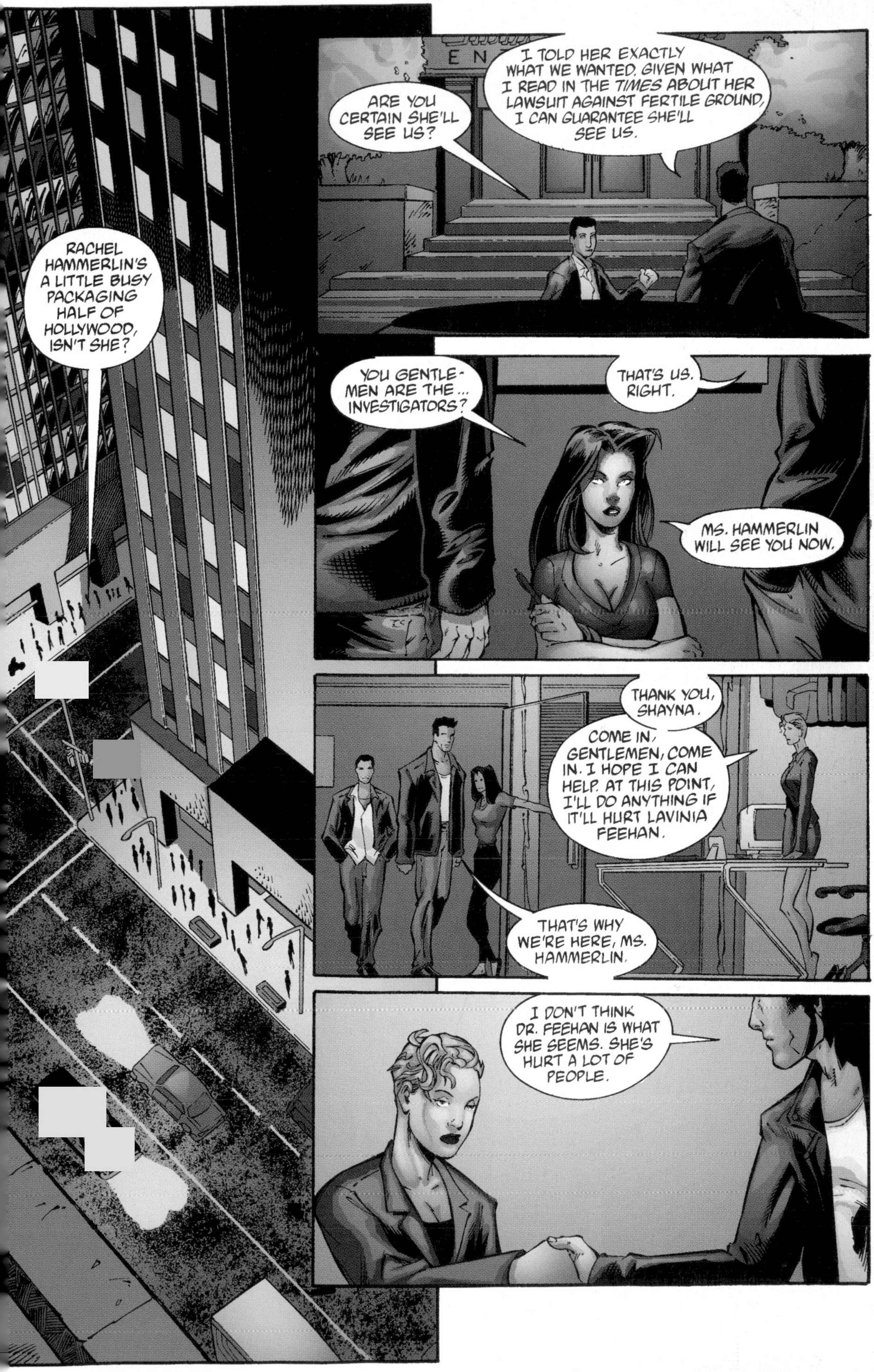
RACHEL HAMMERLIN'S A LITTLE BUSY PACKAGING HALF OF HOLLYWOOD, ISN'T SHE?
ARE YOU CERTAIN SHE'LL SEE US?
I TOLD HER EXACTLY WHAT WE WANTED. GIVEN WHAT I READ IN THE *TIMES* ABOUT HER LAWSUIT AGAINST FERTILE GROUND, I CAN GUARANTEE SHE'LL SEE US.
YOU GENTLE-MEN ARE THE... INVESTIGATORS?
THAT'S US. RIGHT.
MS. HAMMERLIN WILL SEE YOU NOW.
THANK YOU, SHAYNA.
COME IN, GENTLEMEN, COME IN. I HOPE I CAN HELP. AT THIS POINT, I'LL DO ANYTHING IF IT'LL HURT LAVINIA FEEHAN.
THAT'S WHY WE'RE HERE, MS. HAMMERLIN.
I DON'T THINK DR. FEEHAN IS WHAT SHE SEEMS. SHE'S HURT A LOT OF PEOPLE.

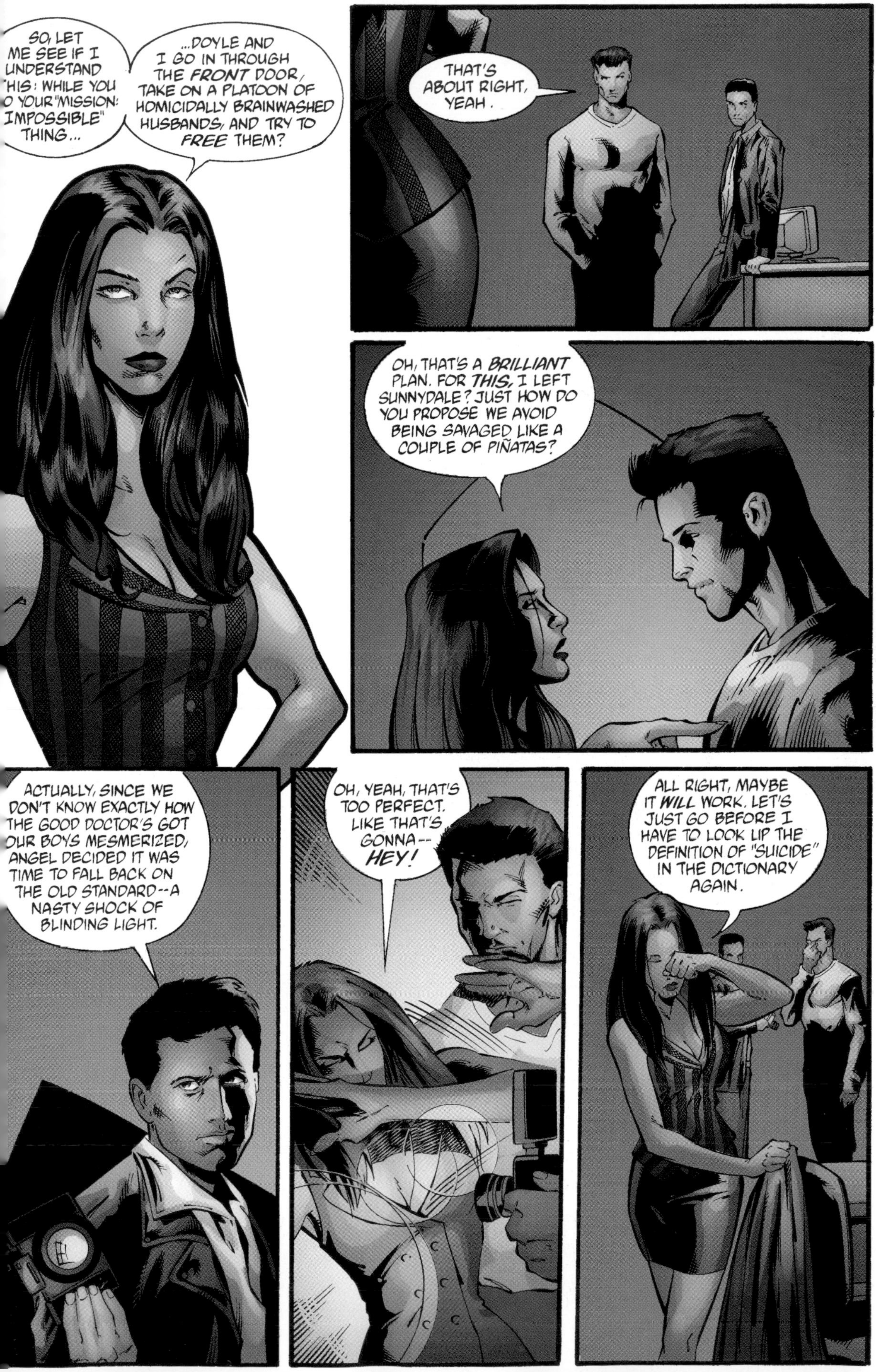
SO, LET ME SEE IF I UNDERSTAND THIS: WHILE YOU DO YOUR "MISSION: IMPOSSIBLE" THING...
...DOYLE AND I GO IN THROUGH THE FRONT DOOR, TAKE ON A PLATOON OF HOMICIDALLY BRAINWASHED HUSBANDS, AND TRY TO FREE THEM?
THAT'S ABOUT RIGHT, YEAH.
OH, THAT'S A BRILLIANT PLAN. FOR THIS, I LEFT SUNNYDALE? JUST HOW DO YOU PROPOSE WE AVOID BEING SAVAGED LIKE A COUPLE OF PIÑATAS?
ACTUALLY, SINCE WE DON'T KNOW EXACTLY HOW THE GOOD DOCTOR'S GOT OUR BOYS MESMERIZED, ANGEL DECIDED IT WAS TIME TO FALL BACK ON THE OLD STANDARD--A NASTY SHOCK OF BLINDING LIGHT.
OH, YEAH, THAT'S TOO PERFECT. LIKE THAT'S GONNA-- HEY!
ALL RIGHT, MAYBE IT WILL WORK. LET'S JUST GO BEFORE I HAVE TO LOOK UP THE DEFINITION OF "SUICIDE" IN THE DICTIONARY AGAIN.

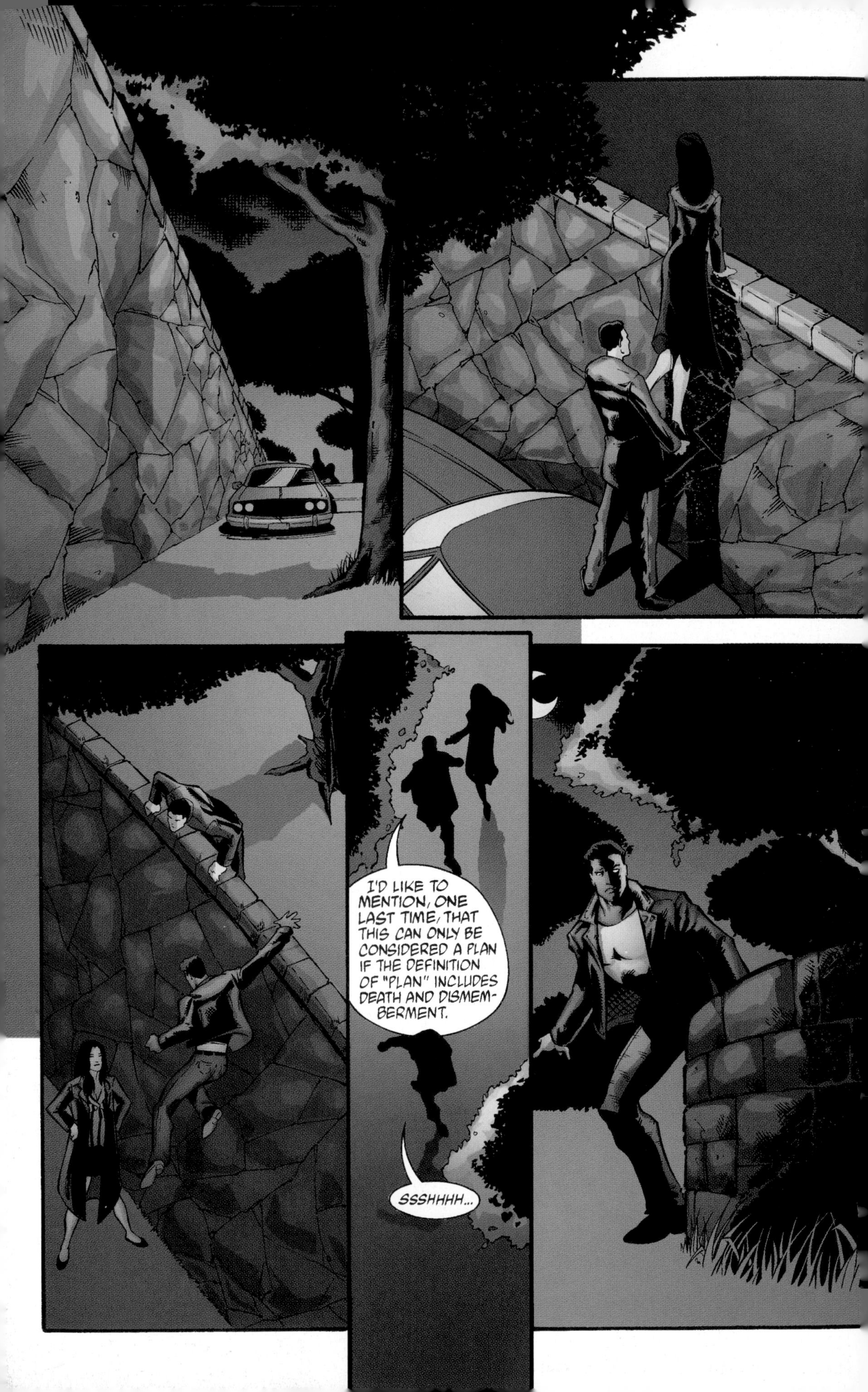
I'D LIKE TO MENTION, ONE LAST TIME, THAT THIS CAN ONLY BE CONSIDERED A PLAN IF THE DEFINITION OF "PLAN" INCLUDES DEATH AND DISMEMBERMENT.
SSSHHHH...

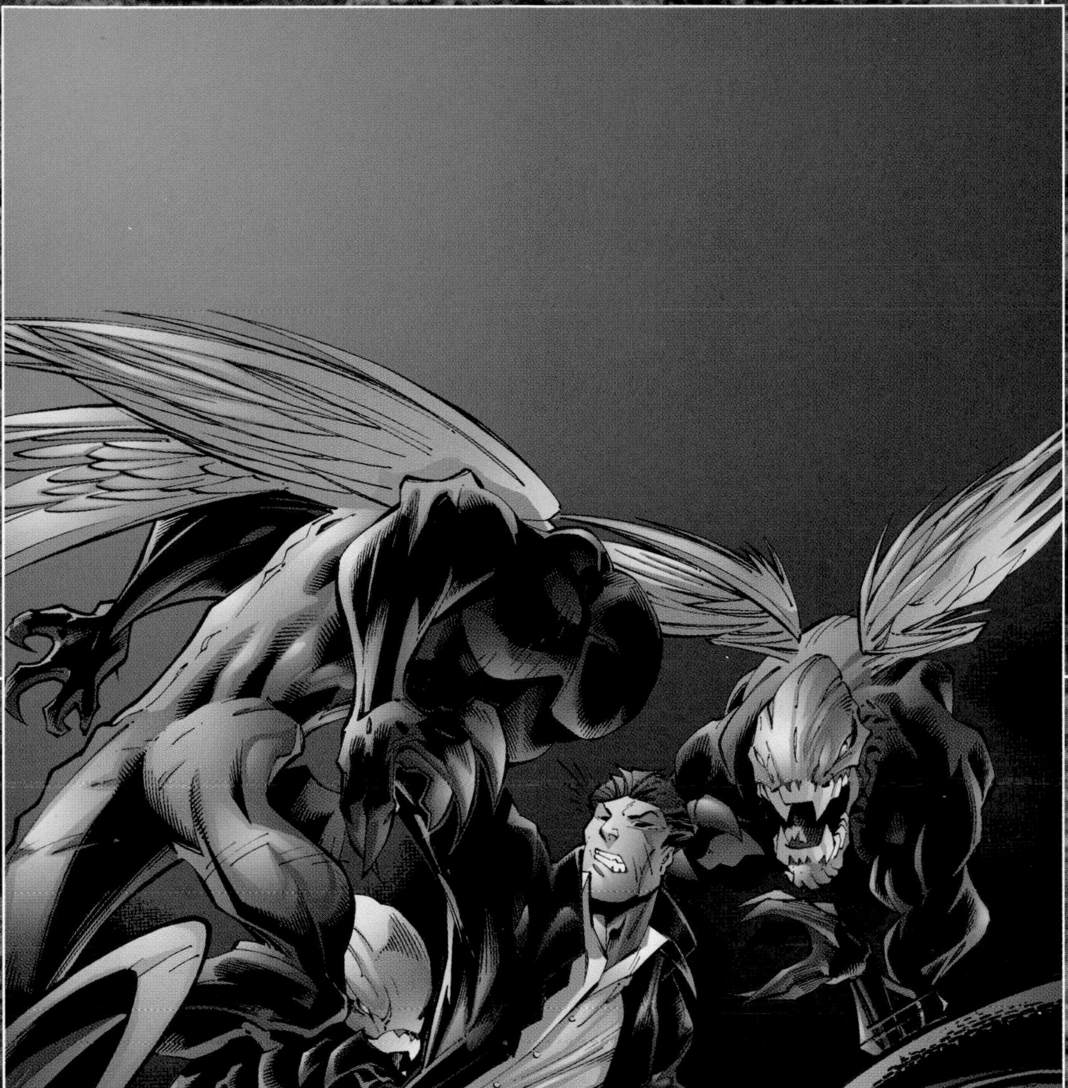

Cover by **Jeff Matsuda** and **Jon Sibal**
Colors by **Guy Major**

Surrogates

Chapter 3

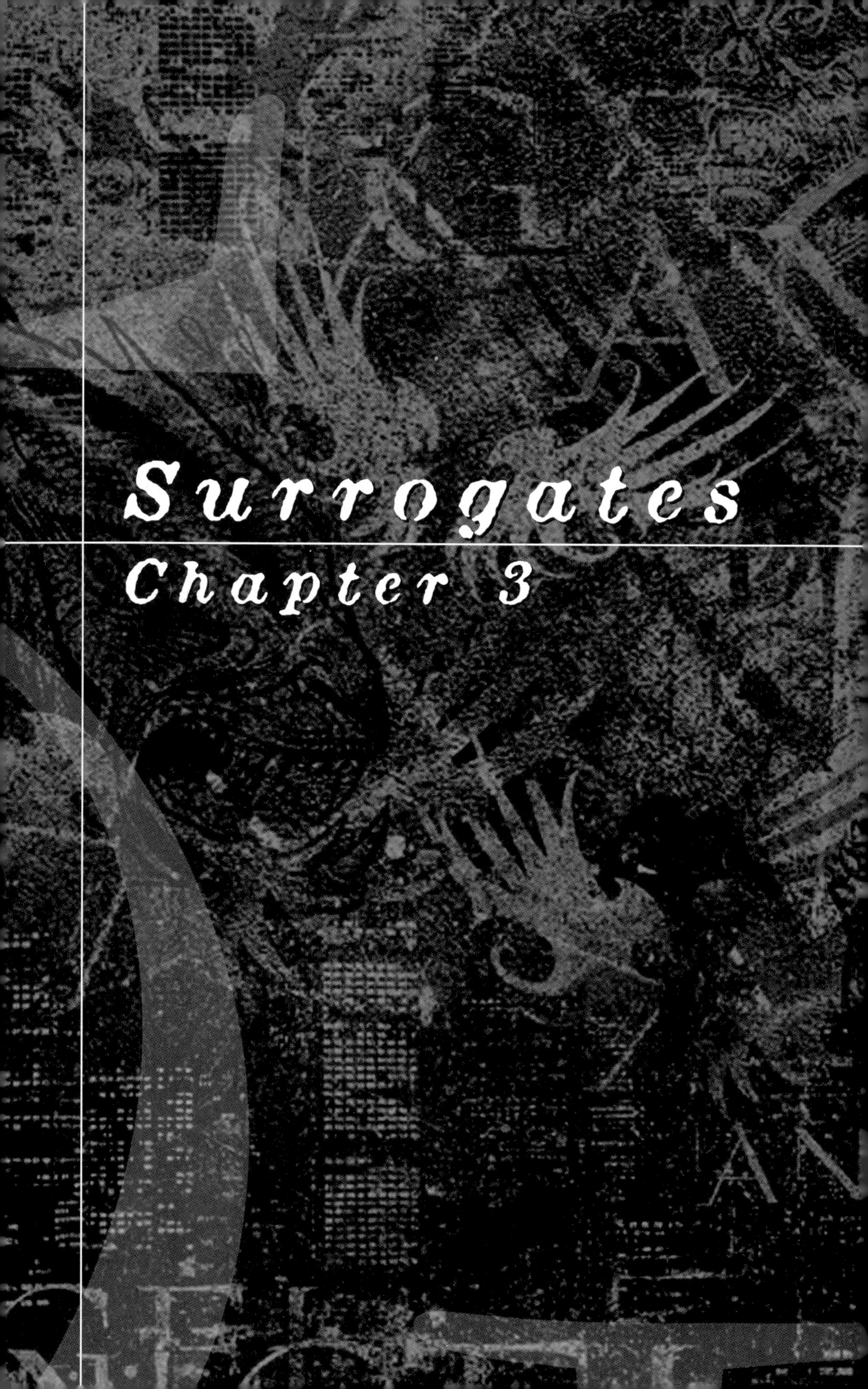

THEY'RE MONSTERS. ANGEL CAN SEE THAT. BUT IN HIS MIND THERE'S THE LINGERING IMAGE OF HUMAN BABIES.

THE PLACE IS CALLED FERTILE GROUND, A CLINIC FOR WOMEN DEALING WITH INFERTILITY. THANKS TO DR. LAVINIA FEEHAN, MANY WOMEN WHO BECAME PATIENTS HERE WERE ABLE TO CONCEIVE.

RITA CARLSON, ANGEL'S CLIENT, WAS AMONG THEM. PROBLEM WAS, WHATEVER RITA GAVE PREMATURE BIRTH TO WASN'T HERS. IT WASN'T HER HUSBAND'S. IT WAS PUT THERE, INSIDE HER.

ONE OF THESE THINGS.

WHATEVER THEY ARE.

RITA HAD A GLIMPSE OF THE TRUTH. AND MAYBE A LITTLE INTUITION AS WELL.

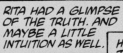

HER HUSBAND, PETER, TRIED TO INVESTIGATE AND DISAPPEARED. RITA KEPT DIGGING AND ENDED UP DEAD.

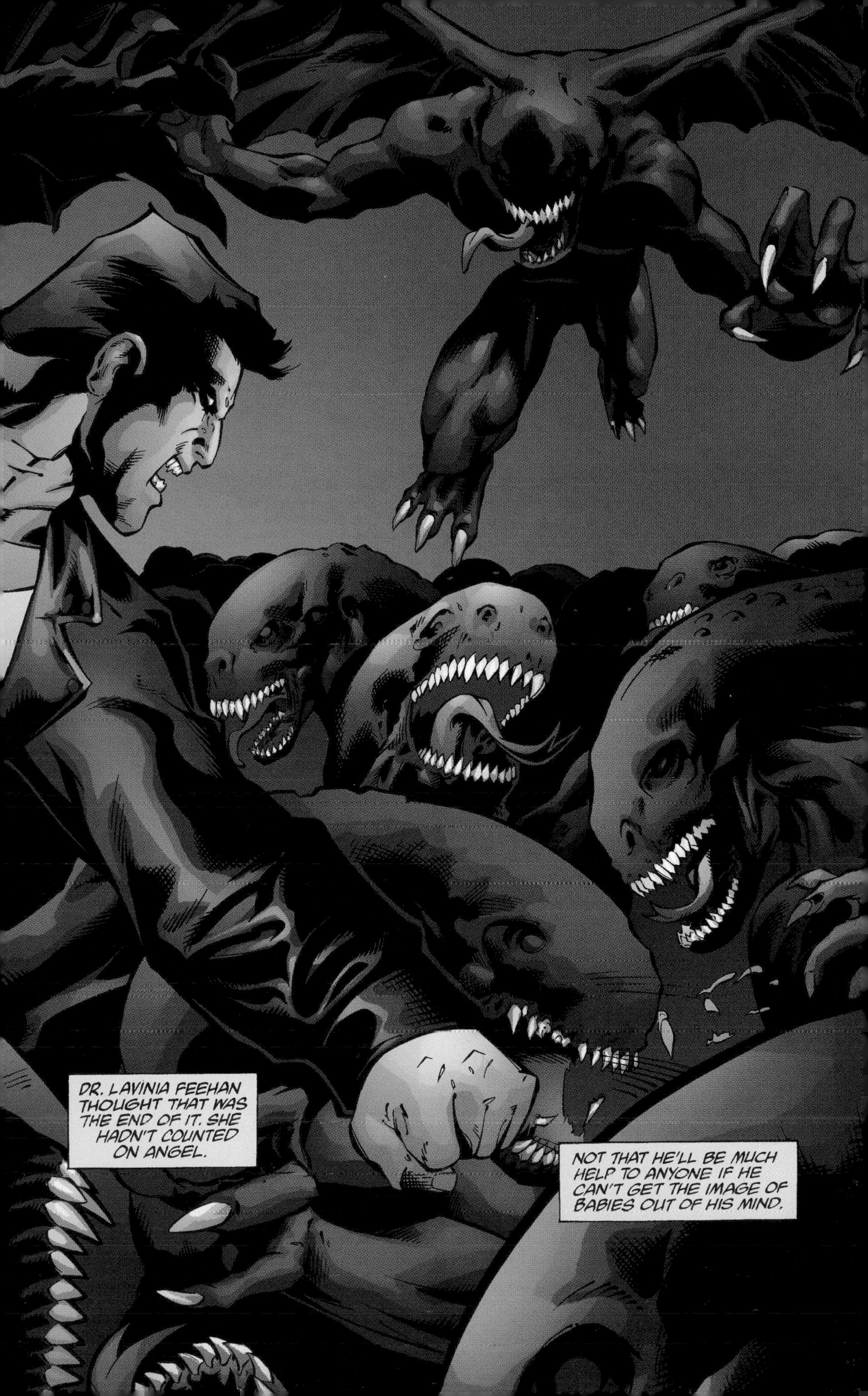
DR. LAVINIA FEEHAN THOUGHT THAT WAS THE END OF IT. SHE HADN'T COUNTED ON ANGEL.
NOT THAT HE'LL BE MUCH HELP TO ANYONE IF HE CAN'T GET THE IMAGE OF BABIES OUT OF HIS MIND.

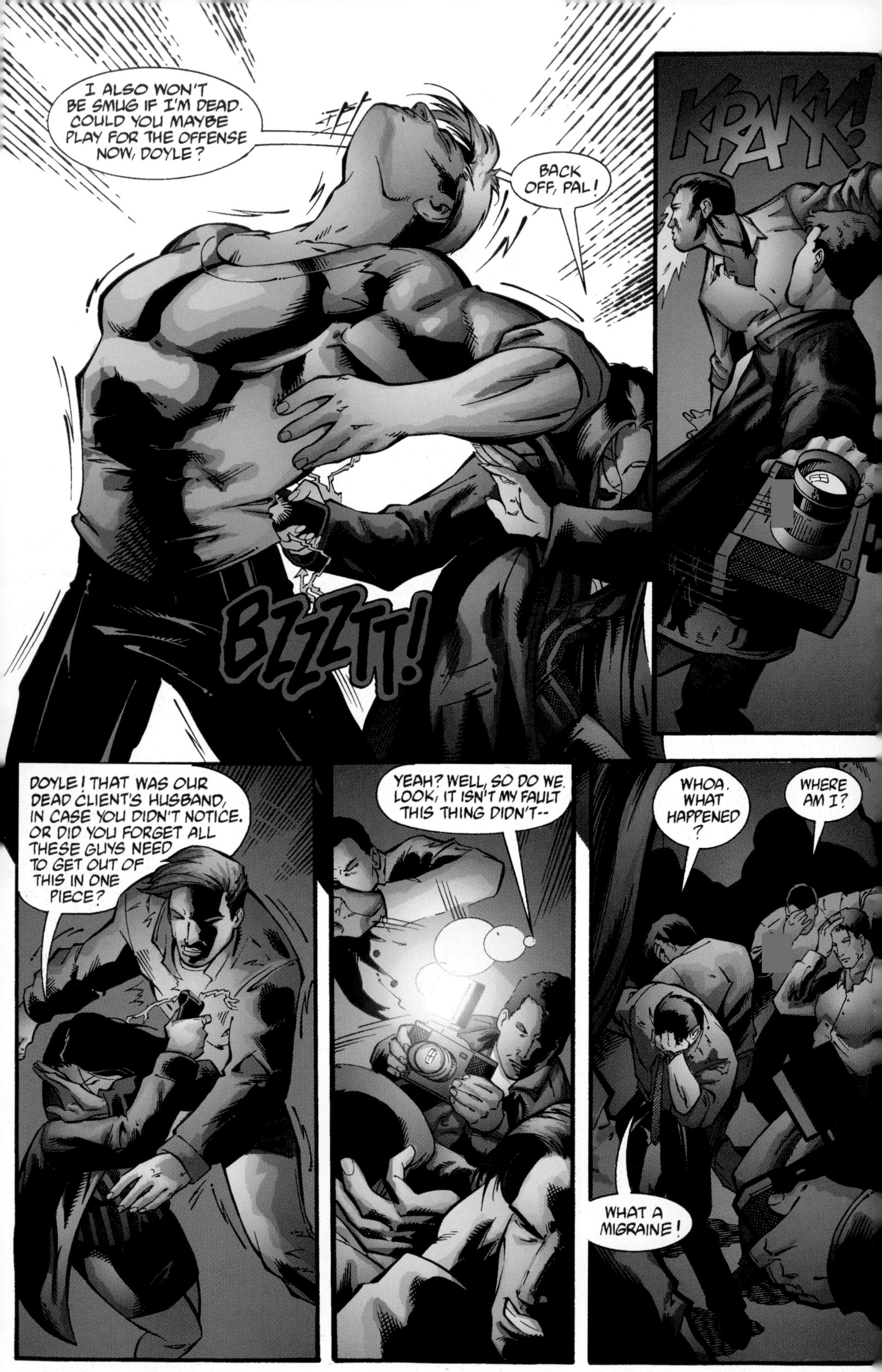
I ALSO WON'T BE SMUG IF I'M DEAD. COULD YOU MAYBE PLAY FOR THE OFFENSE NOW, DOYLE?
BACK OFF, PAL!
BZZZTT!
KRAKK! KRAKK!
DOYLE! THAT WAS OUR DEAD CLIENT'S HUSBAND, IN CASE YOU DIDN'T NOTICE. OR DID YOU FORGET ALL THESE GUYS NEED TO GET OUT OF THIS IN ONE PIECE?
YEAH? WELL, SO DO WE. LOOK, IT ISN'T MY FAULT THIS THING DIDN'T--
WHOA. WHAT HAPPENED?
WHERE AM I?
WHAT A MIGRAINE!

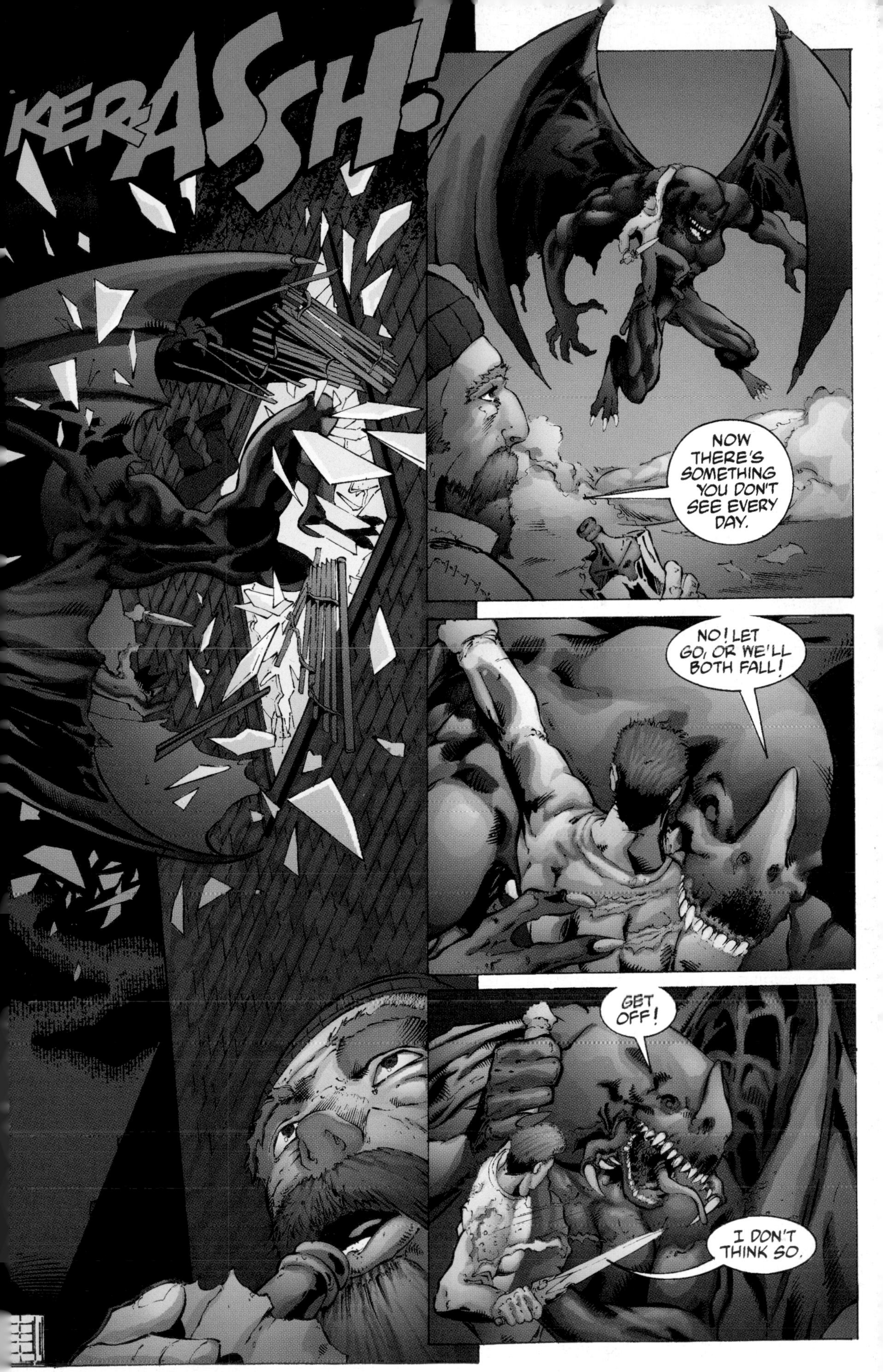
KERASH!
NOW THERE'S SOMETHING YOU DON'T SEE EVERY DAY.
NO! LET GO, OR WE'LL BOTH FALL!
GET OFF!
I DON'T THINK SO.

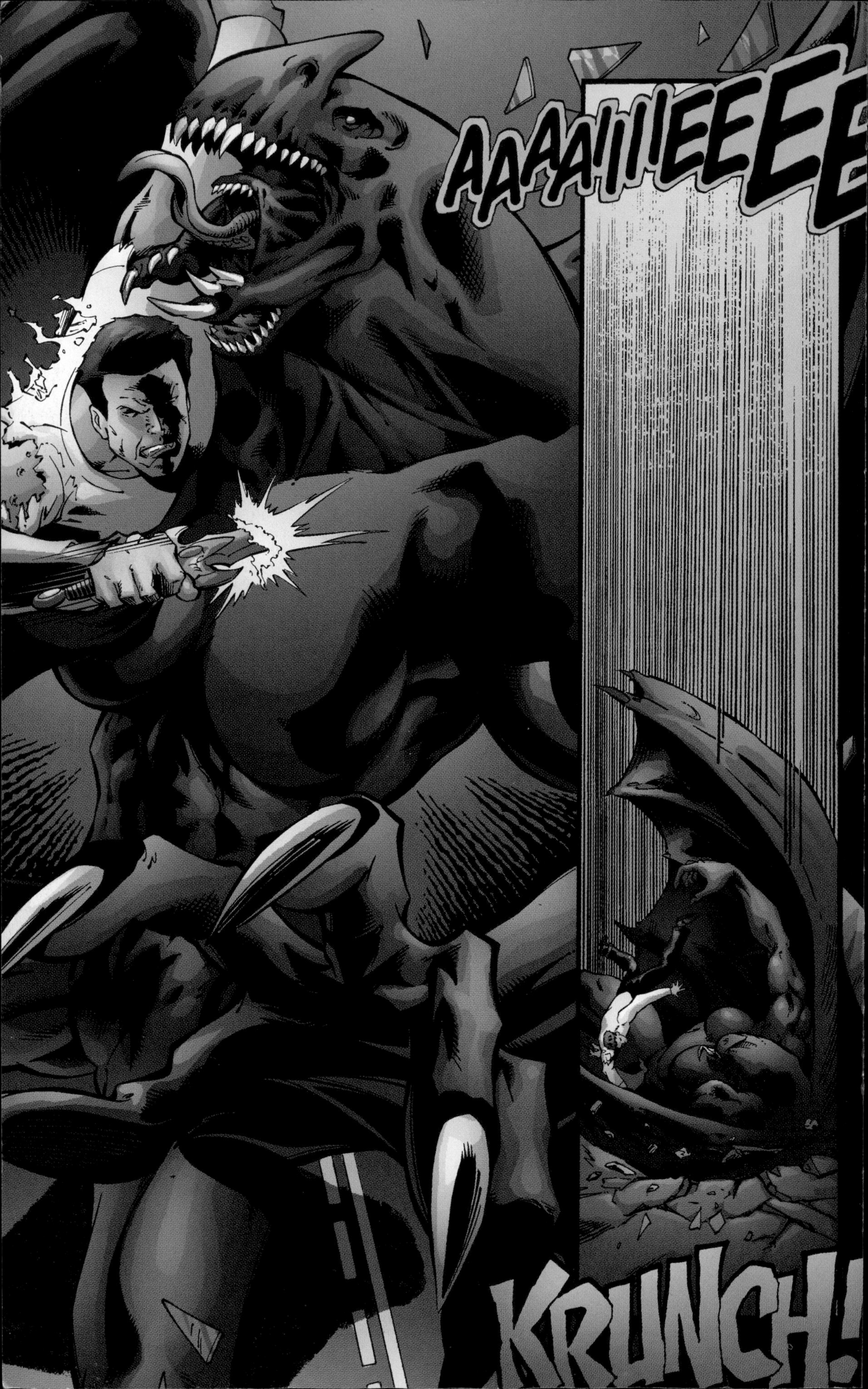
AAAAIIIIEEEE
KRUNCH!

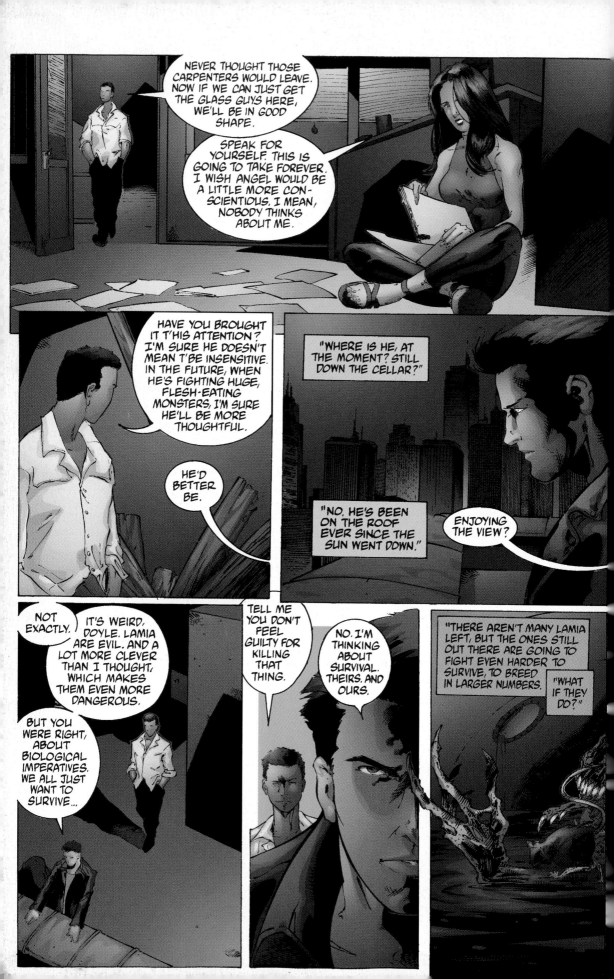

An afterword
by CHRISTOPHER GOLDEN

By the time Dark Horse decided to do a monthly comic book based on the new *Angel* television series that was being spun off from *Buffy the Vampire Slayer*, I had already written the *Angel* miniseries *The Hollower*. Apparently the Powers That Be up at Dark Horse liked that story well enough, because they asked me to write the monthly as well.

Needless to say, I was pleased. Great characters come along a lot less frequently than we imagine.

So, grateful, yes, but also a bit uneasy. The job presented us all with certain challenges. With only a vague notion of what the new status quo was going to be for the series, we had to get a couple of plots approved so we could move forward. The idea was that the basic stories would be approved, and as we learned more, and received scripts to read, and perhaps even saw an episode or two, we'd fill in all the holes.

Well, it's all a bit of a blur to me now, I confess, but suffice to say that when *Angel* #1 was being written, we had seen nothing more than a rough draft of the script to the first episode of the series (which was decidedly not the version that ended up on the air). We had the gist, and that was going to have to be enough.

Fortunately, with the aid of *Angel* merchandising queen Caroline Kallas and Fox Licensing's Debbie Olshan, editor Scott Allie and I had a direct link to the producers of *Angel*. They didn't just read the first-issue script we gave them, they went over it with a fine-tooth comb.

Now, maybe you're thinking that would bother the team on the comics. The truth of the matter is, it was a godsend. Since the TV series was only just being born itself, we desperately needed the feedback we received from the producers. I think it helped a great deal in the development of this first story arc, *Surrogates*, of which I'm very proud.

Christian Zanier has done an amazing job of capturing the mood of the series and the characters themselves. Not an easy task, particularly in these three issues, when we had so little to go on. I'm particularly pleased with what Christian brought to *this* story, which had been percolating in the back of my mind for years by the time I got a chance to write it.

Rule one for writers: don't ever throw away a good idea. There'll come a time when you will find a place for it. So it was with *Surrogates*. Way back in 1991, when I was the Licensing Manager for *Billboard* magazine, I started a short story called "Post Partum" that I never finished. It was about a man who comes to believe his wife's hysterical post-partum claims that her baby was stolen from her at birth and replaced with a duplicate, and goes to investigate.

I never went any further with it, but the story never really left my mind, roiling around back there with a dozen others I'll find a way to use one of these days. As soon as I sat down to come up with ideas for *Angel*, it came back to me. Add magic and monsters, and suddenly the story was not only perfect for *Angel*, but worked better than it ever had in its original form. Immodest as it may seem, I like to believe *Surrogates* has a bit more depth to it than your average comic-book media tie-in, particularly for a first issue.

I also think it's really creepy, this idea that the baby you're coddling and cooing to might not be your own. Something insidious about that. I find it chilling.

I hope you did, too.

--CHRISTOPHER GOLDEN,
Bradford, MA, 2000

CHRISTOPHER GOLDEN is the award-winning, *L.A. Times* bestselling author of such novels as *Strangewood* and *Of Saints and Shadows,* and a teen-oriented thriller series whose titles include *Body Bags* and *Thief of Hearts.* He has written eight *Buffy the Vampire Slayer* novels (seven with Nancy Holder), including the upcoming *Sins of the Father.* His comic-book work has included *Wolverine/Punisher, The Crow, Spider-Man Unlimited,* and many *Buffy*-related projects. As a pop-culture journalist, he has co-written such books as *Buffy the Vampire Slayer: The Watcher's Guide* and *The Stephen King Universe* and won the Bram Stoker Award for editing *CUT! Horror Writers on Horror Film.* Please visit him at www.christophergolden.com.

CHRISTIAN ZANIER was born December 27, 1971 and has been collecting comics since he was five. Like most kids Christian wanted to draw comics, and eventually he went to Sheriden College (in Canada) for a year and half, only to discover it wasn't his cup of tea, and quit. He then started his journey into comics.

Along with a few friends, including comic artists Ken Lashley and Marvin Mariano, Christian opened up the studio Draxhall Jump Entertainment. During his time there, Christian met Randy Stradley, who was then looking for an artist to revive Dark Horse's *Ghost.* Randy liked Christian's samples and gave him the job. Ten issues later Christian asked if he could move over to the world of *Buffy.* Randy talked to *Buffy*-verse editor, Scott Allie, and, viola, the rest is history.

Christian is currently working on *Angel* for Dark Horse and *Rising Stars* for Top Cow.

ANDY OWENS was born and raised in Spokane, Washington. He broke into the comic-book field in 1995 as an assistant to some top professionals. After several years of this "slave labor," he struck out on his own. In the past few years he has worked on such titles as *X-Men*, *Wolverine*, and *Magneto* for Marvel Comics. He has also worked for Top Cow comics on such titles as *Tomb Raider/Witchblade*, *Ascension*, and *The Darkness.*

In the last year, he has worked for Dark Horse comics on *Buffy the Vampire Slayer* and its spinoff title, *Angel.*